THANK GOD FOR GOLIATH

Thank God for Goliath

Turning a Death Sentence Into a Victory Parade

Moses S. Asamoah, Jr.

Dedication

*To every man and woman of God seeking to please God alone and find
yourself in a broken, betrayed and abandoned state. Be encouraged.
Use this book as a blanket as you go through your healing journey.
I found my story in the life of King David, before he
became King. It is my goal and prayer that you find your
story, your voice and your deliverance in mine.
There is a parade awaiting you because you will be
triumphant; you will arise! Cheering for you!*

Contents

Acknowledgments

FOR THOSE WHO may be losing or have completely lost their confidence, be encouraged because God specializes in revival and restoration. You are still important to the Kingdom of God. Get well soon.

I want to especially thank my former Pastor for everything he taught me during my time spent with him. He gave me the opportunity of a lifetime, for that I would always be eternally grateful.

I express my sincerest gratitude to Bishop Courtney McBath for being a father to me when I desperately needed one. Thank you for caring for the Samaritan when I was left for almost dead. You made "son" mean something valuable again. I pray the grace of God to continue to do for others what you have done for me.

1

A Mighty Oak Has Fallen

H E NEVER SAID, but I knew it. The other said it, so I believed it. Both men were evident pillars and sources of hope and identity in my life. I always spoke glowingly of them, though I knew of their shortcomings as much as or more than others. It felt like betrayal if I mentioned one and not the other. So, in my first book, "Sweetly Broken," I acknowledged them both.

For now, let me tell you about these two mighty men in my life. The first one I have known all my life. He named me, and yes, named me after himself. I have always been proud of that. From a very tender age I have looked up to him and wanted so much to impress him. Impress I did, at least that's how he made me feel. My natural father was always present in my life. He encouraged, invested, disciplined, loved and motivated me. Everything he did was great. Those who know me well know I am my father's son. I speak well of him because as a young boy growing up, he was my example.

He was an example and human representation of my Heavenly Father. We all unconsciously learn about God through the relationship with our natural father that we had or did not have. Whether good or bad we picture and understand our Spiritual God through the lenses of our natural fathers. Their actions represent God's thoughts of us. As unfortunate as it may be sometimes, fathers carry the unenviable position of being God in the life of a child until the age where they can distinguish the two. If the wrong foundation is built, it remains or takes a long and difficult life process to tear down and rebuild. My wife once told our oldest daughter that Jesus would heal her "boo-boo," but she responded, "No, Daddy would make me feel better." In her eyes, I was invincible, all powerful and all knowing. Thankfully this pressure will be lifted off me as she grows older but until then, I have the responsibility to reflect God the Father and introduce her to Him when she begins to understand such things.

I never questioned God's love because I never questioned my natural father's love. He demonstrated his love by the continued sacrifices he made for my siblings and me. Even when he did not have a job, I remember he found money to purchase some text books I desperately needed for school. In times when I did not need, he still gave. It was difficult for the family to make ends meet but he was committed to investing in my education. One of the most memorable examples of his demonstrated sacrifice was when he drove about 20 miles from his job to my school to rectify a grading error by my teacher. I tear up every time I think about this story. My previous grade was not bad, but he knew I had worked hard and deserved to be rewarded. He knew how much I wanted to impress him, and this was his way of paying me back. He never told me, but the teacher did. He never told me, but I knew.

I knew that my traveling so far away across the ocean from Ghana to the United States was hard for my father. He grieved and lamented because he would miss me and wondered how I would fare so far away from his protection and provision. I was a young boy finding my way through manhood with a call of God on my life. How would I do in a land of new weather, food, people and schools?

It was during this search for destiny, identity and calling that I met my other father. Our first encounter was so powerful that I can never forget it. I was no longer a young boy. It was 2004, I was now a young man, graduated college and pursuing my Master's degree. Degrees aside, I was still searching for who I was and my place in life, especially in the divine plan of God. I needed guidance, I needed to be grounded, I needed stability, and I needed a father. I heard him speak to the crowd and I liked the way he taught the word of God. It was clear, accurate and it challenged me in my walk with Jesus. Later on during the service, he had several words of knowledge, sharing details of people's life he would never know unless God revealed it to him. Two of those descriptions fit me so well I knew they were about me. I looked around to see if others would respond but no one else did. They were about me.

I responded and went forward as he requested whenever a revelation applied to you. He prayed for me and gave me prophetic words of what God was going to do in my life. I was humbled by what God was saying and counted it a privilege that He would choose me to do that in His kingdom. I came back for the Sunday service and was even more excited by the teaching of the Word of the God. Ezra is my favorite personality in the Bible, and I identify with him because Bible says, "He studied the word of God, lived it and taught it" (Ezra 7:10). I love the word of God and concluded that my church search was over because I found a place and a man of God who actually taught it without the fluffiness and without delusion. This man became my spiritual father from then on.

I served as a youth worker at the church and played on the worship team. In about two weeks, I became the youth leader, an answer to a passionate prayer that I wanted to serve the youth wherever God led me. I saw all the confirmations coming together. I concluded that this must be the place, the church, the man of God I was supposed to serve until it was time to be released into ministry "on my own." I soon quit my job at the Christian Broadcasting Network as a prayer counselor and transitioned on to be my Pastor's ministry assistant. I considered it an honor that he would bring me along to teach me. Our starkly different backgrounds, cultures and mannerisms were evidence that only God could have orchestrated this partnership. I was excited to find a home, a place to serve and grow, and a father who would guide me in this journey of fulfilling my call in the Kingdom of God.

I remember the times he would ask me to join him to go for an appointment or to get something for the church. As we drove through town we talked. Our conversations were not doctrinal but about life and especially the life of being a minister. We joked and laughed a lot...a lot. I remember he asked me to join him on one of his out of town ministry assignments in Ohio. He drove there with his family, and I flew there after school work was done, timing our arrival to within a couple of days of each other. We prepared ourselves for the evening service. In the waiting room before we left to go to the sanctuary we prayed. Then we started to laugh about something silly, and we just lost it. We laughed so hard we were holding our bellies from the pain. Soon it was time to go into the sanctuary for worship. Such moments were so frequent and memorable.

It was also during one of these trips that I had one of my most powerful deliverances ever. My spiritual father was preparing to minister to the leaders of the church in the evening prior to speaking to the entire church the following morning. We got to the home of the host, a church leader, and after the usual pleasantries, we gathered everyone together. As was my custom, while he ministered, I separated myself to pray for him and for God to touch the people. As I prayed, fear gripped me. I became afraid and wondered what would happen if my Pastor ran out of prophetic words to encourage each person. That would be bad, and what would we do if that occurred?

It was then that God spoke to me and said that I was bound by the spirit of poverty. I was afraid there would not be enough to go around. As it is with poverty, you must get what you want, gather as much as you want as fast as you can. Tomorrow was not promised to be good, so today was the day to gather, spend, waste, enjoy what you had. The poverty mentality is always afraid of not having enough or running out of supply. It also results in mismanagement and never truly responsibly saving for the future. It's a "let's eat, for tomorrow we die" (Isaiah 22:13) disposition. God delivered me from the spirit of poverty and assured me that He is the God of more than enough. He would never run out because He is both the Source and the Creator. Thank you, Lord!

I knew God was All-sufficient but this deliverance was gradual. For example, I noticed how I lived my entire life without learning how to create a budget, and then actually live by it. I had to curtail my careless spending and prepare for tomorrow's expenses. There was no need to consume all I had today for fear that I would not have enough for the next day. Ironically, the opposite was true. God is my Provider so I could have what I needed today and trust God that I would not lack tomorrow. I have since learned to budget effectively and be faithful not only with my finances but in all areas of my life. My Heavenly Father delivered me from poverty and taught me how to prosper and live responsively.

Naturally, I carried some of my expectations from my natural father to my spiritual father. In many ways, I was dependent on both of them to shape my experience and understanding of life, people and leadership. I learned how to be disciplined, to be responsible and to have fortitude in the face of adversity. I could never control people or situations, but I could determine my responses. Both natural and spiritual fathers taught me how to maneuver the difficult times that life presented; however, nothing prepared me for the tumult that was about to hit my life when it came to these two men.

My natural father suffered a mini-stroke, which prevented him using the right side of his body. He could neither speak nor write. Suddenly, an independent man became dependent on those around him. Imagine losing your ability to walk, talk, eat properly or control your bowels. Any one of these at the minimal degree is highly uncomfortable, but these, plus other ailments together at one time, was difficult for my dad. The thought of what he was going through was painful to my heart. It was more apparent when I called to talk to him on the phone. The once talkative and gregarious father could now barely utter a word. He responded with grunts and sounds of *agyeiii*, which is translated *ouch!* He wanted to speak so much that it hurt him to be unable to. I cried every time we spoke because I was trying to console him and let him know it was okay. I remember telling him that he had raised a man of God and that everything he needed to do and say to me, he already had. I assured him that I remember every counsel and teaching moment. I would never forget anything he said to me. Truthfully, picking up the phone to call him was extremely difficult for me. I could not bear the pain he went through. I could not handle the fact that I could not hear my father's voice and laughter again. Losing that felt like flying without one wing. The man who I wanted to impress could not affirm me and let me know how proud he was of me. The man who sacrificed so much for me could give no more and there was nothing I could do about it. How I wished I could hold his hand and help him cross over like he always did for me. I was helpless and could only give myself to prayer.

During this time that I was struggling with the failing health of my natural father, the relationship between my Pastor and me was doing well. The church was very supportive in this season. The church was also doing very well. We were growing, had moved to a new building and there was continual movement. Overseeing constant renovation of the building while leading the people spiritually was a challenge that stretched us both. By this point, I had been promoted from Ministry Assistant to Youth Pastor, to Senior Associate Pastor, to now Executive Pastor. I was fully committed to assisting my spiritual father. I submitted what God had revealed to me about my future with his vision and felt comfortable doing that. Why leave to reinvent the wheel when it was happening with him? "Synergy," my Divinity counselor Howard Foltz would say, "is important to complete the Great Commission." If someone is already doing what you are doing, unless otherwise directed by God, join them. Two are better than one for they have a good reward for their labor (Ecclesiastes 4:9).

Soon, the financial weight introduced by this new facility, in addition to other cracks in the armor, began to strain our relationship. It was as if our Batman and Robin relationship suffered a mini-stroke. Trust became a major issue. I could tell that though my Pastor gave the impression that he trusted me, he really was not fully invested in that. There were times where he would ask me questions about situations I had not informed him about. I wondered if I didn't inform him, how he found out something as personal as my schedule. To make matters worse, he was miles away in Germany. He also began to frequently question my decisions, something he never did before. I was so devastated I felt again I had been asked to fly on one wing. Was I no longer the favored and beloved son? It escalated to direct instructions to stand down and that the "captain was now in charge of the ship." I was prohibited from entering certain offices and shut out of meetings I was supposed to be in. The writing was on the wall. Just like my natural father, I felt like I could no longer speak. I was bleeding inside and all I could say was *agyeiii*. The death blow was soon to follow. I came to the church a young man both in life and in my understanding of church dynamics and leadership. After eight years, I was not an expert but I had learned quite a bit. At the very least, I knew this church better than anyone else, next to my spiritual father. The very wings of bold leadership and conviction were now seen as threatening and not submissive. When I graduated from a yes man to a contributing leader to the team it was received as rebellion. The growth in me was that it was no longer my spiritual father's church, it was God's church. If I had to take a stand, it would be for my Heavenly Father above the wishes of both my natural and spiritual father. That was not welcome. Within a week of informing my Pastor that I felt God leading me to plant another church, the hammer, ax, machete and guillotine all fell on me. I was terminated from my position as Executive Pastor, effective, immediately. I was instructed to stay away from current church members and to make sure my church plant was several miles away. I asked to be officially released in front of the church on a Sunday morning.

It was the most awkward experience. Ironically, I was back in the pews where it all started. My Pastor called me forward and said the appropriate things so as not to create dissension among the people. The prayer was half-hearted, I know. I knew it was not genuine because he placed his left hand on my hand while praying for me. Culturally for me, that was a taboo. The left hand in Ghanaian culture is customarily associated with filth since we are trained to clean ourselves with the left hand after using the bathroom. Using the left hand is considered rude and disrespectful when receiving or giving something to another. When I saw the left hand on my head, it took all the self-control in me not to move his hands away.

Spiritually, I consider that a slap in the face. The right hand in the Bible is compared to power, authority and affirmation. It was evident that none of these were intended to pass on to me. After what was clearly a reluctant prayer, I left the church the same way I had come in eight years ago: unknown, disconnected and wondering what the future held. The days and weeks to follow were torture. I was without a spiritual father, a church home and a job.

Disillusioned was an understatement. After some inaccurate Facebook posts and text messages from my former Pastor, my heart was officially crushed. It was in the presence of God that I kept myself sane. I had resolved that no matter what, I would always keep a soft heart. The kingdom of God was more important than a man; more important than my hurts. At the time of the writing of this book, I have neither ran into nor spoken to him since I left the church. It was as if all these years never happened.

A year and a half later, on my way from prayer meeting at Living Destiny Church, I got this text at 9:30pm from my sister in Ghana: "A mighty oak has fallen." I knew exactly what that meant. Stunned and numb, tears ran freely down my face. I knew I would never hear the voice of Daddy again - not even the grunts and ouches. He passed into eternal glory on August 16, 2014. I went, as I was able, to Ghana for his funeral. I went all the way to the cemetery. When they poured the sand over his casket, my heart sunk. Dada, as I affectionately called him, was gone forever. Below is an excerpt of my eulogy to my dad:

"Adjusting to life in America without you was not easy being it was an unfamiliar environment, weather, food, way of life, etc. We talked often and you always encouraged me. One thing you never failed to mention was your instruction to me to always remain humble. Humility you said was the way to success and life fulfillment. I took your advice and would continually live on that wisdom.

You came to America to visit us. You came to my university and I gave you a tour of the campus. I remember well as you examined the building and the various structures. I could see your mind computing all the various aspects of such a project. It reminded me of the long nights and early mornings I would see you working with blueprints and working hard for us. Thank you!

There were two conversations you and I had when you came to America that have forever changed me. I told you of some difficulties I was having, and before you gave me counsel, you listened and proceeded to teach me a song. It was the Ewe version of Isaiah 54:10: "Though the mountains be shaken and the hills be removed, yet my unfailing love for you would not be shaken nor My covenant of peace be removed, says the Lord who has compassion on you." You told me that a long journey does not go beyond its destination and to hold on, and that whatever it was would soon pass. It did! Thank you!

I wanted to make you proud and become a medical doctor to take care of you and have money to provide for your needs. You liked that and looked forward to seeing me in the white robe with a stethoscope around my neck. When the Lord called me into ministry, while in the university, it was right before you arrived in America. It was difficult to share it with you, but I had to. You heard me, kept quiet, went upstairs and after a few minutes came back to me. You said: "Selorm, you have always been good at everything you did. Whatever you choose to do, go all the way and be the best at it." The comfort I felt and the assurance I needed that you would still be proud of me was clear in your words. It was difficult to take that step of faith, but your validation lifted the weight off. If there was anyone else apart from God that I cared to impress, it was you Dada. Daddy is still proud of me! Thank you!

You never met my children, but they will know of you and your mighty deeds. I will live my life in honor of you because you taught me who a father is. I will miss the nights of tea while watching the boxing show Legendary Fights, or our Saturday rendezvous with Football Made in Germany. I will miss you yell out my name when the news was about to be over and Sports Highlights was next. I will miss your broad smile and energetic laughter. I will miss your wisdom and your gentle spirit. I will miss you calling my name. I will miss seeing the love in your eyes. I will miss you dearly!

You have passed on to meet our Lord Jesus. I would see you again. Your body may have breathed its last, but I know I am standing on the shoulders of a giant, you! Giant heart, giant love, giant compassion! Thank you for giving me your name. I promise I will bear it well and continue to make you proud. Keep smiling on me, dada!

Rest in Peace, Perfect Peace! Till we meet again, Dada, I love you!"

When Mighty Oaks Fall

Many have experienced the loss of a natural father, spiritual father or both. The loss of a natural father is obviously not the same for everyone. A range of factors contribute to whether, in your estimation, he was a good father or not. Was he present? Were things bad but got better at the end? Did things never get better? Do you miss him or are you angry at him? Is he still living but dead to you? Do these questions and thoughts and feelings flood your mind as you think about your natural father. Though our reactions to the word "father" are different, they all bear a common denominator. Our fathers are important to who we are. Your father story may not be glamorous, but do not get defensive and protective about being self-made and not needing him. He may have been absent, but his impact is undeniable.

There is an unquestionable impact that fathers have on their children – for good or for evil. I have almost fully recovered from losing my fathers, but I know there's still more work to be done in me. I am healing and functioning well, but I still have open wounds and memories. It is easy to hold on to the joys of my natural father and the time we had together. I must make myself remember the good days with my spiritual father because the separation was so sudden and severe. When mighty oaks fall, the sound and impact reverberates for a long time, sometimes for several generations.

2

PROCESSING MY PAIN

"It is good for me that I was afflicted, that I may learn Your statutes." Psalm 119:71

MANY YEARS AGO, I meditated on this verse and began to see what we have called affliction, abuse or unfair treatment in an unusual way. The heart of man is desperately wicked (Jeremiah17:9) and God's thoughts towards us are to give us a better future (Jeremiah 29:11). God always loves and man is always finding a way to take advantage of, or over another. With that in mind, I embraced whatever situation that I had gone through knowing that God loved me. If a friend or foe was trying to hurt or destroy me, it would still work out for my good. It is good that I went through the things I did. It is good that you went through the horrible treatment that you did, IF and only IF you used it to draw closer to God. Otherwise you became angrier, bitter, unforgiving and distrusting. The experiences were never fun and if it were possible, I wished those cups would pass from me.

"When you pass through the waters, I would be with you; And through the rivers, they would not overflow you. When you walk through the fire, you would not be scorched, Nor would the flame burn you." Isaiah 43:2

I want to encourage you that your pain was and is real; it was unrighteous, unjust and undeserved. The experiences we all want to forget are hurtful and unfair, but if we parked right there, our lives will remain unfruitful and incapacitated. Moving past failure, oppression and depression is what makes you a champion. I challenge you to take the next most ridiculous step and say "Thank God for what I went through". It makes no logical sense and seems downright psychotic, but so is the love, plan and destiny that God has for you. His intentions towards you overpower every trauma you have experienced. When you embrace His love, and declare that in all things you will give thanks, situations will change and conform to the words that you speak. If I may ask, "What can separate you from the love of God? Shall persecution, backbiting, being lied on, cheated, used and abused, forgotten and abandoned, separate you from the love of God?" I speak prophetically into your life that NOTHING, good or bad, can separate you from the love of God.

The death of my father was difficult because I obviously did not want to lose him. Nonetheless, it is the way of all the earth, so I was mentally and emotionally prepared, or so I thought. The impact was devastating and I still have moments of heavy weeping when I think of him. It was easier to handle because he had lived life, was 85 years old, and his physical ailments were so unbearable for me I could imagine how and what he felt. It was easier than the separation that occurred between my spiritual father and me. That was unexpected, unforeseen and totally damaging to me. It was the most confused I had ever been. This relationship was supposed to last many more years. Even if we were to go on to other godly assignments, I always wanted to be able to come home, rest, talk to my spiritual father and then continue on my journey. But this silence was deafening, this severance was crippling.

> *"For it is not an enemy who reproaches me, Then I could bear it; Nor is it one who hates me who has exalted himself against me, Then I could hide myself from him. But it is you, a man my equal, My companion and my familiar friend; We who had sweet fellowship together Walked in the house of God in the throng."* Psalm 55:12-14

I want to take you on this journey of what I went through and how I overcame. I pray that you find your story in my story, process the pain and receive the strength and grace to climb out, fight through and overcome in Jesus name!

No one is perfect. We all have faults, so I want to preface that what I am about to share with you is not to paint my former spiritual father in a bad light. This is my part of the story and how I felt and how I overcame. I am the man of God I am today because he gave me the opportunity to serve when others merely acknowledged me from a distance. I learned a lot under his leadership and unashamedly use some of the principles he taught and displayed. I choose to look fondly at our experience before it went sour and say, "Thank you Lord for everything I learned."

I thank God for teaching me biblical accountability. Before I was unceremoniously laid off, several situations arose that I believed required intervention from those we were accountable to as church leaders. With each situation, I realized that there was no account-ability; as my Pastor used to say, "It's good to be king" - he was king. No one had the authority to correct him and whatever he wanted was final. This was so in all areas - leadership, financial, administratively, etc. I looked back and I saw the serious error in that structure. When there is no one to correct, or rebuke a leader, eventually he becomes a god in his own eyes. There is good reason why the United States government is set up with the checks and balances among the Executive, Legislative and Judicial branches. There is safety in accountability.

There is also humility in accountability because when a leader has genuine accountability, he is humbled by the opportunity to serve. He knows it is not a right but a privilege. It takes humility to admit that you are human and that the tendency to seek absolute power is naturally strong. Because we know we would be tempted to cut everyone out of our lives and have our own way, we must immediately submit our lives to those who have authority to challenge us and if necessary stop us to save us from ourselves.

Who are you accountable to? Who is willing to tell you the truth no matter how it makes you feel? Who have you given permission to question and challenge your integrity, commitment and follow through?

When my loyalty was questioned, I thank God that He did not allow me to defend myself.

"He was oppressed and He was afflicted, Yet He did not open His mouth; Like a lamb that is led to slaughter, And like a sheep that is silent before its shearers, So He did not open His mouth."
Isaiah 53:7

This was the instruction of the Lord before my last two meetings with my former Pastor. In those meetings, I was chastised, talked down to and told I would not succeed. I was blamed for trying to cause division in the church and that I was not loyal. Many years later

God vindicated me. The point here is that you must learn to let God defend you. When you try to defend yourself, it is usually not received and sometimes you cause more damage in an attempt to right the wrong that is done to you. I am glad I kept my mouth shut.

People have said things and believed things said about you that were far removed from the truth. It is annoying and hurtful when those who you knew would not believe you but choose to believe the lie. It is difficult when God does not allow you to give them "a piece of your mind." I highly discourage giving people a piece of your mind because after several times of giving, there would be little or nothing left for you. Let God defend you. If he appointed you, no one can disappoint you! Let them talk and slander for your God will surely arise and protect your name. You are His child and He takes it personally when people come against you.

I do not fear what man can do against me because my heart is to serve Jesus. I have noticed that I am faithful to a fault. You may have realized that about yourself as well. Even in the face of complete disaster, we still find a reason not to abandon ship and hold on to whatever hope there might be left. When others left without reason, I stayed without reason except the reason that God had not released me yet. My commitment to faithfulness required me to stay through thick and thin. I can boldly say that I did not run away from the situation and that I had nothing else to give. Of course, God does not want us to be faithful even to the point that we ignore or do not hear His voice. The voice of God has become the only thing that moves me or makes me continue in a situation, no matter how successful or dreadful. My faithfulness to a fault has made me a better Pastor. I do not give up on people easily. When I commit to serve you, I am with you all the way regardless of your response. Unless God says otherwise, I am committed to minister to you. My fault, in the eyes of some people, is when I continue to communicate positively when the response if unfriendly, abusive or unfavorable. When I believe in you, I believe in you. There is no fault in that, is there?

I thank God for my insecurities and inadequacies. I am a very confident person who is very comfortable with who I am. I am hardly moved by the way people think of me. Surely I want it to be favorable, but I do not need them to know my self-worth. For a long while, I heard the voice of my former Pastor in my head. He had said I was a good preacher but was unable to lead a congregation. It stuck with me and stunk on me so much I had to pray it off. I became insecure and unsure of every step I took. I wondered when things were slow whether I had truly heard God and could do it. As I spent time with God, I became confident again.

Tapes may be replaying in your head, the voices saying: "Who do you think you are?" "You are just like you mother/father!" "What makes you think you can make it?" Those dream busters are real, and your mind is too quick replay them. Renew your mind with the Word of God until you believe what He says about you. I am grateful that my Pastor discouraged me and said I could not make it because it made me very cautious and deliberate in building an effective team around me. I learned not to possess the church but to serve it. I learned to ask for wisdom when I needed it. I am not afraid to ask questions because I feel I have so much to learn and do. Feeling inferior because of insecurities is not of God. Instead being humble and teachable is the way to overcome insecurities and inadequacies.

After a situation like mine, you can become angry and unforgiving. Don't do that. You must embrace the difficulties and grow by them. As I reflected on my story, I confronted and was forced to deal with three spirits. Obtaining victory over the spirit of Rejection, the Vagabond spirit and the spirit of Absalom, was important for my deliverance. Let's look at each one of them.

THE SPIRIT OF REJECTION

When those you love act in an ungodly manner, rejection begins to show its ugly head. The spirit of rejection takes root when a person repeatedly feels left out. Many people carry this deep-rooted problem from their childhood. If not dealt with, it can carry over into other relationships, especially marriage.

Rejection is at its worst when you begin to expect to be rejected. With a preconceived expectation that you will be rejected, you isolate yourself and judge yourself badly. Before you meet and know people you already decide they do not like you and thus you cannot relate to them. Prejudice against yourself is a symptom of the spirit of rejection.

10 FRUITS OF A SPIRIT OF REJECTION AT WORK IN YOUR LIFE (ADAPTED FROM AANDBCOUNSELING.COM)

- You find yourself comparing your circumstances or situations with others, and you never seem to measure up.
- You feel like you missed out on life's opportunities and now it's too late.
- No amount of encouragement is enough to convince you of your worth.
- You feel rejected if you are not greeted or acknowledged by leadership.
- You constantly seek the approval of others and suffer from people pleasing.
- You are easily offended or embarrassed from discipline or correction.
- You are always trying to prove yourself in public.
- You feel like you are on the outside looking in during interactions with people.

- You think you could do a better job than the current leader or teacher if you are given the opportunity.
- You believe no one understands you, or what you are going through.

I overcame being rejected with the confidence that God loved me no matter what and by continually declaring and expecting the favor of God. I am so favored that it is unusual for me if I do not receive favor. I expect favor instead of rejection. I expect to be received well. There is something about you that is attractive and admirable. Some people would never see it; ignore them. Others would see it, embrace you and encourage you. That is your tribe. Understand that some may never understand you and therefore reject you, but that is not because of you. You are special and wonderfully made. It is a loss for anyone who rejects you because they are truly missing out. Those people include you. Love yourself.

Jesus said in the Great Commandment that we should love our neighbor like ourselves. Focus your attention first on yourself, not your neighbor. It is selfish, but rather important, because if you hate yourself, you will hate your neighbor. If you receive only fifty percent of yourself, that is how you will love your neighbor. Love who God has made you; stop rejecting yourself, and you will have the love of God to share with others. Stop expecting rejection. Look for favor because indeed you are favored of the Lord! My first, middle and last name is FAVOR. My friend, call me favor. I call you favored, in Jesus name.

MAKE THESE DECLARATIONS:

- I am favored of the Lord.
- Everywhere I go, I am well received and honored.

- I am may be rejected by man, but I am always favored by God.
- I command the spirit of rejection to lose its hold over me in Jesus' name.
- Every painful experience that triggers rejection be exposed and healed in Jesus' name.
- I forgive those who have rejected me and made me feel unwanted.
- My value is from the being accepted by Jesus; all others are secondary.
- Lord heal the pain in my heart. I surrender it all to you.
- Lord, teach me how to love and receive love in Jesus' name.
- Help me to see love, even in rejection, in Jesus, name.

One thing I am certain of is that because of my extreme loyalty, I had to experience what I did to push me out of my comfort zone and familiar territory. I was enjoying where I was, and God used rejection to provoke a move in me. I did not understand it then, but I do now. See rejection through the eyes of God. He always loves you and will never leave you. Living Destiny Church is the fruit of my rejection. Thank you, Lord!

Many prominent men of God were rejected: Moses (chased out of Egypt), Joseph (put in a pit and sold into slavery by this brothers), Jephthah (kicked out of his father's home because his mother was a prostitute), Paul (upon his conversion, the early church did not believe it and were suspicious), David (chased out by King Saul to the land of his enemies, the Philistine's) and our chief example Jesus Christ. Ever felt rejected? You are in good company. Find the plan of God in the rejection. Do not look back at what you lost, but use the freedom to move toward what God has set ahead of you. Rejection hurts, but it defines your next step by sifting the company you keep. The stone that the builders rejected has become the chief cornerstone. May you prosper in your season of rejection and blossom beautifully wherever God leads you.

THE VAGABOND SPIRIT

Rejection is in close fellowship with abandonment, and that partnership invites a distant cousin called the Vagabond Spirit. A vagabond is defined as a person who wanders from place to place without a home or job. My situation was a perfect setup to be a victim of this spirit. I could have become critical and suspicious of all church leaders, trusting of none. That would have led to never settling down in a home. Having no home is actually a state of fatherlessness.

Many Christians suffer from the bondage of this spirit. Church hurt has kept them from wanting to trust any church leader, or anybody, for that matter. If they are consistent in a church, they never commit or settle and are quick to move on at the slightest image that reminds them of their previous experience. Beyond the church application, the vagabond spirit keeps people from settling down in any relationship or job. They keep changing jobs and exiting relationships as soon as it requires commitment. The vagabond spirit keeps you in constant motion around the mountain making sure you never reach your promised destiny. I declare that the power of the vagabond spirit be broken off your life in Jesus name. You will build and plant and eat the good of the land in Jesus name!

I refused to be a spiritual vagabond because that makes me open to attacks of the devil. I also understand divine authority, submission and accountability. I could not be in authority if I was not under authority. Leaders are human and should one fail you, forgive them and put another in their place. My quests for a father - one who understood me, would help heal my wounds, and give me family to belong to - led me to Bishop Courtney McBath. It was a God-directed encounter in the mall that led to a meeting that has me under his covering today. The story about how God restored me and planted me quickly is amazing.

I met with Bishop McBath when I was totally broken and did not know who I was and what I was worth in the ministry. He heard my story and was very sympathetic. He understood because he had been through a similar situation. Friend, you are not alone. Bishop began to pray for me and said,: "Father, restore his confidence." I broke down in tears, not knowing until that point that I had lost all confidence. I had been told I would not make it and was believing that lie. On my way out, with my face shaped by my tears, he said, "I am proud of you, Son." If you remember how I love my natural father and how I served my former Pastor, you would understand that having a father was more important to me than being a leader. Fatherhood means identity, belonging, inheritance. It means home! At that point I broke down again. I am amazed at how God has given me a home and planted me so quickly. May the Lord plant you and give you a home in Jesus name. You will not wander from place to place, church to church, job to job, relationship to relationship in Jesus name!

THE ABSALOM SPIRIT

Absalom was the oldest son of King David. After returning from exile, Absalom began coveting his father's throne. He sat at the entrance of the king's court and began judging the people's cases instead of allowing them to go see his father. The Bible says he gradually began to win the hearts of the people of Israel. He turned their attention from the true king to himself. Absalom eventually declared himself king, chased his father out of town, and sat on his throne. In the end, he was killed while fleeing the battle with King David's men.

I share this with you because I understood the dangers of circumventing leadership a long time ago. Unless you are appointed by God, your coup will not last.

"A man can receive only what is given him from heaven." John 3:27.

You cannot have what belongs to another person. I guarded my heart against being an Absalom and never once invited people to follow me rather than the God-appointed leader. Yet, that was exactly what I was accused of. It hurts, but vindication is of the Lord.

Watch out for Absalom creeping up in your heart. Because of pain, it is easy to become judgmental of church leaders. Nothing they do meets your standards. Absalom arrives when you now feel you can do better than those put in authority over you. It gets worse when you try to get a following away from another man to yourself. It involves lying, overpromising, and a lot of flattery for people to follow you. If you must lie and cheat to lead, are you truly the leader? God, not you, is the judge of that.

Whether it is as a leader or follower, you cannot allow the spirit of Absalom to direct your affairs. Stay in your lane!

The few things I have shared about my experience are to encourage you to embrace the processing of your pain. Begin to see a horrendous moment as raw material for God to create something greater and better in your life. There is some good in rejection. May you see God through any affliction you have or are experiencing today!

3

THE WRITING ON THE WALL

"He came unto His own, but His own received Him not..."
John 1:12

REJECTION IS DIFFICULT to handle for anyone because, by nature as human beings we all want to belong. We know not everyone will accept us, and we do not fit everywhere, but we believe and expect that there is at least one place where we can call home and be ourselves, that place where we do not have fear of condemnation or criticism.

The author of Hebrews describes Jesus as our High Priest who is not ignorant of our experiences, pains, fears and burdens:

"For we do not have a high priest who is unable to empathize with our weaknesses, but we have one who has been tempted in every way, just as we are--yet he did not sin." Hebrews 4:15.

Jesus himself went through the emotions you and I go through. He understands. When you are rejected in the place you call home, the nail drives deeper and the sorrow is much heavier. As if for shortness of breath, you feel you can no longer live. What is there to live for, and where is there to go? That may be your story after years of investment and sacrifice in that place you called home. Suddenly, like lightning, the place where you are honored and respected is gone. You are the villain. You are no longer welcome.

If you are like me, I would sometimes look for old pictures or drive by the church locations as if to feel normal again. Maybe the positive experiences that occurred in those places would give me hope to continue. The memories were vivid and torturing as well because I could not go in. I was still not welcome. You hope like the prodigal son, from a distance, your father would run and say welcome home. But the closer you got to "home," the further it felt and the more you were faced with the certainty that it truly was over. Do not weep, servant of the Lord, your vindication will come. Your Father still smiles on you!

Many years ago, when activities at the church were at their peak, I was speaking to one of my friends who was moved greatly in the gift of prophesy. It was a great conversation, but something he said is forever imbedded in my mind. He told me that I am called to be a leader and that my Pastor would eventually let me go. In my mind, I reasoned that it could not be true. I prayed that it would not be. I reasoned again that if it was so, my leaving would be akin to the triumphant entry of Jesus into Jerusalem, with shouts of celebration. It was not so. God was trying to prepare me for what He had in store for me. It was not for the wrong that would be done to me, rather the right that God has planned for me.

When we spend our time trying to figure out who did or would do us dirty, we lose sight of the preparation process we must engage in to be where God wants us. Judas or no Judas, the cross was the way of salvation and the plan of God. To fulfill all prophetic declarations in the Word of God, Jesus would have to go the way of the cross. Your destiny is established and prophesied in the plans of God. Stop looking for ways to avoid it. Stop guessing who it would be. Like Jesus, we are *"fixing our eyes on Jesus, the pioneer and Perfecter of faith. For the joy set before him he endured the cross, scorning its shame, and sat down at the right hand of the throne of God"* (Hebrews 12:2). Your promise is greater than the pit, your blessing greater than the betrayal.

Five years went by, and these times were not glorious. The writings on the wall were beginning to thicken, and the warnings were getting louder and louder. Many people began to leave the church, but I am Moses, the old faithful. I would stay until I am the last because that is what I was supposed to do. And practically, I had invested too much of my time, strength and effort to go somewhere and start all over. I was hanging on until a renaissance took place. It was too costly just to leave. I was the co-pilot, and I was staying.

My wife had a dream where a building was on fire and people were trying to find their way out. People were screaming and finding the exits to the building. During this chaos, my wife saw me with a bucket of water running towards the fire. I was not trying to leave. By God, I was going to save the building by any means necessary. It wasn't until the building began caving in that I began to run towards the door. I got out before the building fell down, but it was clear that I had given my best effort to save it. When she told me this dream, I listened and my chest tightened. God was clearly warning us of what was to come. I reasoned again and prayed for rain to put out the fire. It cannot end like this, Lord, it must not!

I too had a dream. In the dream there were two desks in an office space. It was very tight in there. I saw my Pastor sitting in one chair and I sitting in another. Picture this: Office space, two desks on the left and right, with both chairs in the middle. When I sat in my chair I would be looking east, and when he sat in his chair he would be facing west. The revelation in the dream was that every time he tried to get out, his chair would bump into me, so I would be forced to go into my table to make enough room for him. The same was for me. When I woke up, I concluded that the same space was too small for both of us, and the only way to make this work was for one of us to leave. It was not surprising who had to leave. It was not my church, and I was the junior officer. God was preparing me!

Without going into all the details, other situations occurred that revealed the displeasure of my Pastor towards me resulting in warnings and restrictions of what I was able to do and places I was able to go. Through it all, my heart hurt, but I did not want to believe it was over. This church was home and when families disagree, they find ways to make it better. It was not to be so.

You may be coming from a relationship where you did not notice the writings on the wall. Maybe you saw and ignored them or hoped to pray the warnings away. Do not blame yourself, for many of God's preparations we do not understand. It is not until we have the experience that we realize what we just went through. Joseph did not understand the venom from his brothers and why they hated him so. He hoped his time in the pit was temporary and that he would get to go home soon where they would work it out as a family. Moses did not understand that forty years in Midian was preparation for 40 more years in the wilderness leading a bunch of rowdy and ungrateful sheep. You were not supposed to see or understand; otherwise you would have run! You ask yourself how you could have missed it. Friend, you were supposed to miss it. God hid it from you in order to finish His work in you. The question you should ask now is "How did I respond in the fire?" If your response was not right, go make it so. If your response was godly, then move forward; you have passed the test.

I believe I passed the test – not with flying colors, by any means. There were moments where my dreams, my pain, and what others were seeing and saying almost crippled me. My enthusiasm was clearly diminished. There were times when I doubted myself and questioned my resolve to keep fighting. I had days when I wanted to run out and be free, but I could not. I smiled, but all who knew me knew it was a front. The Bible captures my feelings in this verse: *"Even in laughter the heart may ache, and rejoicing may end in grief"* (Proverbs 14:13). My emotions and zeal were clearly affected. In those cases, I was human. So were you! You hurt, you cried, you grieved over the situation and hoped the pain would all go away. You wished you could go back to the good days and be a family again. I am sorry, it did not happen that way for us.

I passed the test because I did not seek to divide and did not lay hands on God's anointed! Even though my emotions were raw and I had all the evidence to justify an accusation or retaliation, I did not. I remembered David who had a prophetic word and anointing to be king after Saul. He found himself in caves, no longer the decorated general of Saul's army. The glory days after Goliath were over. The banquets at the king's palace had ended. What went wrong? Why did I not see this coming? Remember, you were not supposed to! In the moment when David's men had located Saul and encouraged David to do justice, he did not. His hunger, bitterness and rejection could have overridden his honor for God and his respect for the kingly position.

David did not touch King Saul because he knew one day, he would be king and whatever he sowed he would reap. Think like a King! Behave like a King! I knew that my future ministry would suffer if I said things against my Pastor. I was not ready to trade a lifetime of God's goodness and favor for a few moments of fleshly gratification and the approval of other men who could not see my destiny. Man's anger does not work the righteousness of God. So whatever you call righteous indignation should not lead you to violate the divine order of God. What you sow you reap. I have sown years of faithful service, and I was not going to allow a season of discomfort rob me of my future. For a year thereafter, I prayed and asked God to reveal and forgive anything I had done or said against the man that would hinder my life and ministry. The kingdom of God is more important than my personal victories. Friend, pass the test!

For those of you granted the gift of prophesy, word of knowledge and the ability to see into the realms of the spirit what is and what is to come, I want to encourage you. You have great responsibilities that come with the gift. Lives can be built up or shattered if the gift is misapplied or carelessly handled. There are three things I would remind you to never forget.

Firstly, God does not put you in charge and void His divine order based on what He has revealed to you. We know in part, and we prophesy in part. So do not let what God has shown you make you over confident, or make you think you are an expert in the situation. For everything He has revealed to you, there are a hundred more things He does not allow you to see. Your insight does not authorize you to disrespect or dishonor the king. Even when a prophet was sent by God to rebuke or correct a king, the prophet still followed divine protocol. Do not permit your excitement or anguish to push you to disobey God's order. What you say may be heard or not. Obey God and leave the rest to Him

Secondly, your assignment is to be the mouthpiece of God. You speak what and when He asks you to. In many instances, God reveals to you months and years ahead of time. If you speak out of turn you will dishonor God. If you add to what He shows you, you make God out to be a liar. Stay tuned to God and let your yes be His yes and your no be His no. The integrity of your gift is crucial to the healing, correction and restoration of many in the body of Christ. Be patient.

Thirdly, God may just want you to pray and not speak about it. You are not required to say everything you see. Prayer is essential when relationships in the body of Christ are turning sour and the enemy seeks an open door to destroy and divide. Pray, pray and pray some more. Let your desire for mercy override the need for justice. Jesus completed justice on the cross for all of us. When a brother or sister in Christ is in the wrong, it is not our place to seek justice. It is our place to seek and pray for mercy. For the grace of God it could be us in their shoes. Mercy!

I recently spoke to my brother in the Lord who was going through the same thing I had gone through. I could relate with him and let him know that I completely understood where he was. I could tell he was relieved to have someone else bear him up during this dark season of his ministry life. I share this with you to encourage you that what you are going through is not uncommon in ministry. Fortunately, or unfortunately, it happens. I encourage you to see God through it all and move on in His power. We talked about Paul and Barnabas. Paul, at the time when he was recent convert to Christianity, was feared by the believers. They did not believe that he was truly saved and feared it was a trap to kill them the same way he had done to other Christians. Barnabas took him in and used his influence to introduce him to the church and calm their fears. Without Barnabas placing his reputation on the line, it would have been relationally difficult for Paul. Fast forward many years, Paul and Barnabas had a falling out and decided to go their separate ways. It was an unpleasant situation. However, God honored both of them on their ministry journeys. Thank God for trouble, because their work was doubled as a result of a disagreement. Division in the body of Christ is ungodly, but God-initiated conflict is not.

Hear me out. Conflict is not division; it is a disagreement of opinions. If handled well, conflict results in growth of all parties involved.

Conflict challenges traditions, and God uses it to introduce His new direction and order for the church. When a new idea meets an old way of doing things, there is conflict. If we as Christians handle conflict as led by the Spirit of God, we will not see conflict as negative, but as a necessary moment in advancing the kingdom.

I never wanted to pastor "my own" church. I enjoyed being number 2. I was in a place of authority and influence without the weight of being the ultimate leader. Senior Pastors go through a lot. Between God and His people, senior Pastor is not a position to be wrestled for. But God had other plans. The writings on the wall were fulfillments of many years of prophesy; and my dark days generated several of such prophesies. Thank God for this trouble, because out of it something living and powerful is born.

Interestingly, I had mentioned to my Pastor six years before I was laid off from the church that we should plant another branch of the church in Norfolk. That was at the peak of the ministry, and I felt we needed to harness the energy and momentum to plant another church. He said no and that he needed me there. I submitted to his decision. Many years later, in my anguish and abandonment, I had a dream about the Norview area in Norfolk. It was clear that Norview was where we were supposed to locate the new church. I had neither pastored in nor learned anything about Norfolk. I was forced to confront my models for ministry and my expectations of ministry. I was no longer going to be second in command over a big church. I was now Senior Pastor of a church beginning from scratch, in an area I knew nothing about. This reminds me of my name sake, Moses, the prince of Egypt. Welcome, my friend, to the new frontier of ministry. You are called and appointed and God will use situations, even the ungodly and unfortunate ones, to push you out into parts unknown to share the gospel with people to whom Christ in unknown. Welcome to kingdom service!

I changed the tires on my 1999 Infiniti G20 recently. I hesitated because of the cost of replacing all four tires. I cringed every time inspection was due and was pleasantly surprised when the tires passed. I was going to keep the old tires until the next heart-wrenching state inspection was due. God said no, change them now. I was disobedient for many weeks until my disobedience caused me to fear for my life. I decided to spend the money and obey God. Two things happened with the new tires on the car: the shaking at over 50 mph stopped and the automatic swinging to the right when I let the steering wheel go also stopped. There was nothing wrong with the engine or interior of the car. The tires were wrong!

We are sometimes faced with difficult decisions that end up moving us from what we have always known. We are familiar with the good, the bad and the ugly of a situation or location, and do not mind nursing the comfort forever. Then, God comes in and says, "Change the tires! Change what you are standing on! Change the instrument that would move you to your destiny!" It's time to change! Child of God, God forced a change in you because there are many more miles ahead of you and the old tires, no matter how faithful they've been, cannot handle the new terrain God is leading you to. It's time to change!

When the shaking stopped, I concluded that what I was standing on determined the faith or the shake! When man is no longer more important than God, your shaking stops. When your disappointments turn because you are standing on the Word of God, his shaking stops. When your destiny is no longer tied to your years of service but to your loyalty to God, your shaking stops. All fear is gone. You are now able to go faster without fear. This change is good for you. Thank God for trouble!

I thought I had a wheel alignment problem, but I did not. There is nothing wrong with your love for God and your relationship with Him. Time has passed, and it is time to change tires. The old tires/ties could not carry you any longer. Your alignment with God is great, I pray. If so, then examine your tires/ties. The conflict you experienced, or are currently having, may be a misalignment of assignments. The church, relationship, leader you are aligned to may have reached their destination when it comes to you. It is time to change tires and move further. If you do not heed the writing on the wall, God may force you out! If that is you, say thank you Lord and move on. Remember, if your response to God's revelations were not godly, please go back and fix it. If it was good, then raise your hands and say thank you, Jesus!

4

ZERO EXPECTATIONS

"I know your deeds, that you are neither cold nor hot. I wish you were either one or the other! So, because you are lukewarm--neither hot nor cold--I am about to spit you out of my mouth."
Revelation 3:15-16

ONE OF THE most difficult things to do after experiencing rejection, abandonment and betrayal is to find balance. Everything in you and around you may have been is thrown out of alignment, so much so that you do not know what to think, how to feel, who to trust, or how to move forward and continue to believe that what God has said to you will come to pass. When your expectation of who God will use, or has been using, to bless you is dashed, there is a sense of hopelessness. You may be experiencing that right now. Don't punish or rebuke yourself for grieving. All the emotions and thoughts can keep you in a place of fluctuating confidence, but guilt will keep you permanently trapped on the wrong side of healing. You have been hurt. You are disappointed. You may have played a little, a lot or no role in it. Forgive yourself, make things right with others, but do not wallow in guilt. It is the plan of the devil to keep you down. Be free, in Jesus name!

Guilt says, "I am the problem," but the Word of God says, "There is no condemnation for those who are in Christ Jesus" (Romans 6:1). You are not condemned; you are forgiven. After a genuine and careful assessment of your heart, you may realize you did nothing wrong and were totally blackballed. In that case, do not allow the thoughts of guilt to linger at all. You are not to answer for someone's misdeeds. Likewise, stop being guilty about not knowing it ahead of time or seeing it coming. Remember, you were not supposed to see it. Guilt is not the healthy response.

It is my firm conviction that my God will not punish me for someone's foolishness. Relationships are the fabric of society, and everything that is done requires depending on or partnering with others. No one is an island. Basically, you need someone to build your house, or make the road or bottle your water, etc. In a nutshell, no matter how independent you claim to be, you are not. On the other hand, co-dependency is unhealthy because another human being becomes God in your life. It is totally unfair and impractical to expect from another human what only God can provide. The weight of carrying another person will eventually overwhelm you. The healthy form of dependency is inter-dependence, where we mutually support each other, but are willing and able to carry the necessary part of our personal lives, with God having His rightful place as our Source. Because of our need for others in our lives, actively or passively, we are affected by other people's actions. The consequence of their actions impacts us. When their decision is unwise and the consequence is painful, we feel it. However, feeling the negative impact of their wrong actions is not a death sentence to the plans of God for your life. You are not doomed to failure because of your affiliation with another person who chose the wrong way. God is merciful and just! Regardless of what someone else does, He will redeem you from the hands of the enemy. Only with your eyes will you see the fall of the wicked. (Scripture Verse?)

I believe in what Mordecai told Queen Esther after his request of her to intervene in the impending destruction of the Jews:

> *"For if you remain silent at this time, relief and deliverance for the Jews will arise from another place, but you and your father's family will perish. And who knows but that you have come to your royal position for such a time as this?"* Esther 4:14

In this instance, the Jews had no voice and their fate was sealed. However, God placed Esther in the palace to be their advocate and voice. God will always make a way for you, even when you are about to bear the consequences for something you did not do. God will speak for and defend you by any means necessary.

God will redeem you from the mess that you came from. You will go through the fire, but you will not be burned. Like Daniel and his friends in Babylon, you will come out of the fire and have no smell of smoke on you. That is how good God is. He delivers us from the wrong judgments of others. If it were not so, we would all have been destroyed.

> *"For just as through the disobedience of the one man the many were made sinners, so also through the obedience of the one man the many will be made righteous."* Romans 5:19

We depend on Jesus for our destiny, our hope, our assurance, our future, our identity, everything! One man's disobedience threatened to destroy mankind, but God said no. If Jesus' obedience saves all who believe from eternal damnation, do you believe that He will also save you from another's person's woeful decisions?

I feared that being let go from the church and being separated from my former Pastor meant my platform for ministry was destroyed. What was my pedigree now? Who is my father? From which home do I come? All these questions are not asked aloud, but they demand internal answers for people who are going to follow you. They want to know who you are. The easiest way to judge someone's character and capability is to find out where they are coming from. That is why we have a heavy dependence on résumés when seeking employment. My résumé was not pretty: Laid off, church relocated, church shut down, people hurt, and you were the Executive Pastor and didn't see this coming? Yeah, like I said, not pretty. Some went as far as saying they did not want that kind of spirit around. As if I was carrying the "spirit of church division and destruction" on me. What do I do now that the very shoulders I hoped to stand upon have thrust me into the desert and into sinking sand? I felt it would have been better had I not been there at all. But that was not true; that was a lie of the enemy! No time there was wasted, and God is my Redeemer. He is my platform, and when I stand upon His word, every plan for my life will come to pass.

As I wrestled with this fear and in seeking to find my platform, I was encouraged by Psalm 66:11-12:

> *"You [God] brought us into the net; You laid an oppressive burden upon our loins. You made men ride over our heads; We went through fire and through water, Yet You brought us out into a place of abundance."*

Praise the Lord! When I studied this verse, my first conclusion was that "You" had to be another human being. God will not do that to us. Then I went back and read the context and understood that it was

God that had brought me to the net, laying oppressive burdens on my back, causing men to ride over my head. God did that. And He also brought me into a place of abundance. The same God who allowed trouble is the same one who blesses with increase. There must be a reason for the fire, water, nets and burdens, so I asked. His response to me? You cannot bring impure things to the new level. All this time, I was blaming another person for my trouble, and God had taken over the reins and decided to use it to purify me. I wanted more, but I also had baggage. God had to take it off. Your baggage includes unforgiveness, pride, rudeness, laziness, selfishness and any of the fruits of the flesh. Look at the situation through the eyes of God and see that He will never leave you nor forsake you. If you are going through this right now, then He wants to remove some things in you that will cripple or kill you later. Pass your test and thank God for trouble!

> *"Consider it all joy, my brethren, when you encounter various trials, knowing that the testing of your faith produces endurance. And let endurance have its perfect result, so that you may be perfect and complete, lacking in nothing." James 1:2-4*

I understand how it feels to go through trials, and believing for the best, and hoping it ends soon but to enjoy it sounds like a stretch. The last thing on anyone's mind is how they intend to endure trials and count it all joy while going through the trouble. The natural response is quite opposite. To have this joyful disposition takes a confident assurance that "all thing work together for my good." Imagine being at the gym and bench pressing some weight. At your desired weight, you are comfortable and know what to do. Out of the blue, someone adds more weights to both sides of the rod. It is a struggle, but you push through it. After a few weeks, that weight is normal to you. The more weights that are added, the more difficult and frustrating it is. But according to James, count it all joy and embrace the pain of more weight because it is making you stronger. The testing is increasing your endurance and capacity. Don't go seeking for trouble, but when a person or situation becomes more weight in your life than you desire, do not complain, just lift it and get stronger.

I must admit that one thing I'm still struggling with is confidence. It was completely shattered in one of my last meetings with my former Pastor. Forget the mental and emotional anguish of dealing with a house on fire and leaving "home." Now, one of the important tools I would need to survive out there was ripped from me. In a nutshell, he felt I was a good preacher, but I would not be able to lead a congregation successfully. He went on to tell me the statistics of failed churches in America. Feeling devastated is an understatement. I knew what God was telling me to do, but I had not been that way before. My former Pastor knew I was new to church planting. He could also tell that I was seeking his blessing and affirmation. He was intent on not giving me any and casually depleting any reserves of confidence that I had. Maybe you would have been stronger; I wasn't.

Truthfully, this revelation did not come to me until I met with Bishop McBath. He listened to me like a father would and then prayed for me. This is how he began his prayer: "Father, restore his confidence..." I knew something was wrong in my heart, but I did not recognize that it was confidence I was lacking. I have overcome a lot of it, but I continually receive prophetic exhortations about confidence. I must need it if God keeps revealing that I do. I am being vulnerable with you, and I need you to be vulnerable and honest with yourself. The painful experience you suffered took something away from you. You can pretend to be all together, but you are not. The sooner you allow God to expose and heal the wound, the better you will be in the long run.

I am much better than I was at the beginning of the process, but I have found myself stopping and second guessing myself. Things that should be easy to decide or believe God for take longer than they should. I have become overly cautious and gun shy. I am sharing my faulty ways of thinking. What are your faulty ways of thinking?

Immediately following the lay off from the church, I came up with one catch phrase or new principle I was going to live by. It went like this: "I have zero expectations of people." The man I expected the most from had taken everything away and done to me the things I least expected him to. Obviously, high expectations were my problem. I told myself that I trusted too easily. It was time to be tough, realistic and not have anyone push me around. Life is not kind to the gentle ones. I went on and on, cementing this new thought in my mind. I reasoned that this would keep me from being disappointed by people.

Disappointment is the measured difference between expectations and actuality. If my expectation level is 9, and you deliver a 6, I have a disappointment level of three. However, if I set my expectation level to zero, and you deliver a five, I am not disappointed at all. I am impressed by five. Sounds like a good plan to avoid the hassle of pain, rejection and abandonment. I even shared this with others as if to say I had solved the world's problems.

I was doing well with it, until one day in prayer, God revealed the hardness of my heart and told me that I was applying the same principle to Him and thereby not working by faith. I did not imagine that I had cut off all expectations of God as well. Without expectations of God, I was declaring that I was not going to let Him hurt me, as if He was going to. In my pain, I was treating God as a foe and not a friend. Not knowing what to do, I asked God to help me. He said to trust people and have expectations of them. If they should hurt me, He would heal me. That was a more practical way to live, otherwise every relationship would be so guarded, any activity would be a suspicious one.

Zero expectations mean zero relationships because every relationship comes with expectations. You cannot be effective in life and in ministry without trusting and having expectations of other people. Should they fail you as some would, trust God to heal your heart and keep you going again. After all, is that not how God relates to us daily?

5

Healed in His Presence

"Then they cried out to the LORD in their trouble; He saved them out of their distresses. He sent His word and healed them, And delivered them from their destructions." Psalm 107:19-20

THE MOST DIFFICULT thing that could happen after the bitter divorce of a relationship of any kind is the willingness and ability of both to try to trust again. After investing so much, the default decision is to never allow the same thing to happen to you again. That means not trying and never trusting again. Don't let that happen to you. If you park your life at the hurt and the pain you will never become the person who God intends for you to be. If you refuse to love or trust again, you limit your potential in life because of something someone else did. What they did was downright ugly and nasty, but there is nothing in this world that should be able to keep you from fulfilling destiny!

The last text message I received from my former Pastor was in response to my inquiry about my last two paychecks. The message was very cutthroat and mean. I chose not to remember or revisit the message, so I deleted it after a few days. I mention it because it was at the moment I nearly violated the instruction, *"Do not touch My anointed ones, And do My prophets no harm"* (Psalm 105:15). I know how you may feel about that. Because they are in the wrong, they are no longer the anointed ones. Be careful not to play God and jump into the judge's seat. They are still human, and God expects them to make mistakes. Their mistakes do not disqualify them. Only God appoints and dethrones. I typed up several harsh responses, but God told me to delete them. I did and then I typed another scathing message, which in my opinion was not as bad as the first. God said to delete that too. I did.

Not being able to retaliate or speak my mind like I wanted made me so helpless. I felt I was being weak and allowing another man to toss me about. I felt the need to defend myself against the wrong accusations and wicked conclusions being drawn about my character and integrity. I heard lies and more lies but could not respond because, like a sheep led to the slaughter, I was not supposed to open my mouth.

I was so confused and disheartened that there was only one thing I could do. That one thing was to run into the presence of God. I took a quick shower. My tears were as much as the water flowing down the shower. I was weak. My strength was gone. There was nothing else to do but to lay down in my bedroom floor and talk with my Heavenly Father. I put on some worship music and cried a lot more. With every thought came a cry. I worshipped, I prayed, I cried, and did it all over again. I went into the presence of God because of two principles I govern my life with. First, the answer to everything in life is in the presence of God. Second, always keep your heart soft because hardened hearts break easier.

THE PRESENCE OF GOD

I am made in the image of God and "in Him I move I have my very being." Our very existence begins in the very presence of God.

> *"Before I formed you in the womb I knew you, and before you were born I consecrated you; I have appointed you a prophet to the nations."* Jeremiah 1:5

God knows your sitting down and your rising up. The same way I read the manufacturer's manual to learn how to operate a piece of equipment, I go to God to understand what I am made of and how I am supposed to function. When things are not going the way you desire or expect, you need to check in with your Creator.

The presence of God is the very manifestation of Him because God is a spirit. We do talk about God's eyes and hands, etc., but that is anthropomorphism. It is basically we humans imposing our physical characteristics on God in a bid to understand and better relate with Him. God is not limited by the things that limit us. His presence is God showing Himself to us. In that case, all I need is the presence of God because that means I always have God with me.

In both my creation and functioning, the presence of God is the full answer to every situation in my life. With God on my side, I am secure and confident that whatever I need will be taken care of. In the same way, a baby longs for its mother for food and protection, so it is when you come to the presence of God. Nothing dramatic. Just you and God – peace, perfect peace. I encourage you to love the presence of God above anything else. Treasure it and consider it your most valuable weapon for success and fulfillment in life. Being in the presence of God is home.

Consider Hebrews 4:10-11: *"For whoever enters God's rest also rests from his own work, just as God did from His. Let us, therefore, make every effort to enter that rest, so that no one will fall by following the same pattern of disobedience."*

The Bible exhorts us to do whatever it takes to get into the presence of God. Fight off anything that is a hinderance to coming in to the presence of God. If you can get there, He will fix whatever is broken. In addition, anything that keeps you from the presence of God must be removed and avoided. Your excuses for not praying and reading your Bible and spending time with God are contributing to the delays, frustrations and the lack of satisfaction in your life. It is said that man can live weeks without food, days without water, and minutes without air, but a second without nerve function. The connection between the brain, the spinal cord and the rest of the body via nerves is the true lifeblood of our bodies. The presence of God is that important. You need it so bad that I beg you to get back into the habit of being in the presence of God. For lack of a better term, we become the walking dead without the presence of GOD. We may be alive in the natural, but dead in all spiritual aspects.

The presence of God is so vital that after King David committed adultery with Bathsheba and had her husband murdered, he prayed this prayer. "Cast me not away from your presence. Take not Your Holy Spirit from me." (Psalm 55:11) In other words, take everything (my kingdom, my money, my fame, etc.) but please do not take the one thing I need, the presence of God. Maybe our lack of respect and appreciation for the presence of God is because we have created other idols to fill the place of God. It is time for you to remove everyone and everything in your life and schedule and put God as the primary source of your joy and strength.

Yes, I know God is everywhere and you are always in communication with Him. However, I consider that taking a dip in the pool; it does not replace a bath. Once or twice a week in church is great. Keep it up, but that too does not replace your time in the presence of God. Try working out your marriage on your drive to work and back and a few moments during the day. Your marriage works based on your intentional investment of effort, emotion, time and intimacy. Maybe the correct question is, "Do you consider your relationship as more important than marriage?" If so, prove it and show up!

The presence of God is the answer to every problem in your life. The pain and resentment you are feeling right now cannot be healed by your counselor or conversations with trusted friends. They are like a dip in the pool—refreshing, but not enough to be the ultimate solution. The words of the song, "In The Presence of Jehovah," by Geron and Becky Davis, says it all:

In and out of situations,
That tug-of-war at me
All day long I struggle
For answers that I need
But then I come into Your presence,
And all my questions become clear
And for this sacred moment,
No doubts can interfere

Find your way to the presence of God by any means necessary. Disappoint people if that's what it takes to connect to your source of life and hope. Truthfully, you are no good to them dead.

ALWAYS KEEP A SOFT HEART

I find it very hard to say sorry, but not because I am always right or think it's above me. Apologizing has this awkward feeling that comes with it. It is so uncomfortable. That is why I try very hard not to say harsh things, even when I am justified in doing so. An eye for and eye does not work because both end up being one-eyed. Before you "have to say something," think of the consequences. When your emotions are raw and you want the other person to hurt as bad as you, there is the temptation to say or do things that leave irreparable damage. You can never take your words back. Multiple apologies help and do heal, but the memory of it takes longer to erase. Save yourself the time of torture. That's not to say you never speak the truth. The secret is to speak the truth in love. In the heat of the moment, you are likely not walking in love, so bridle your tongue until your heart is healed and whole again.

I restrained myself from responding to the texts. I held myself back from "blasting" him. I was angry and embittered. And then I remembered it was more important for me to keep a soft heart than to be right. With every thought and emotion, my heart was invited to get harder and wicked. Friend, a hardened heart does not happen overnight. It results from a continual abuse of your mind and emotions to the point that you can no longer stand it. A hardened heart is kept hard by very good reasons. Your hardened heart is based on valid, documented and real reasons. However, there are consequences.

A hardened heart no longer has a regular heartbeat. An irregular heartbeat disrupts the flow of blood and could result in blood clots and stroke. There is a negative impact on the entire body when the heart is off beat. In spiritual terms, an irregular heartbeat affects your relationship with the rest of the body. You become unpredictable in your actions and emotions. Some days, you are excited and fun, and the next moment, you hate church and don't want anyone around you. You begin to feel and sense things that are not there. Even if they are present, you exaggerate them because your sensitivity is irregular.

A hardened heart cannot receive from others. Not only is the blood flow from a hardened heart irregular and unpredictable, the constricted passages prevent blood intake. When you have a hardened heart, you are suspicious of what everyone gives you for fear that it is a trap to hurt you or to take something from you. You end up with little or no inner circle of friends, and those who are lucky to be that close suffer your continued mistrust and testing. You are forced to live only on what you can get for yourself without depending on others. Remember, we are made to be interdependent, but a hardened heart defends the independence. Unfortunately, this is the independence that makes hermits out of people.

A hardened heart is set in its way. If you allow your heart to be hardened, you will always have to be right. The hardness of heart prevents all malleability. It is either your way or the highway. People "never understand you," and you decide that either they need to agree with you or the relationship is over. One of the primary types of evidence that a heart is healing from hardness is the willingness to change and let others "win."

A hardened heart does not allow, nay, cannot allow, itself to love again. The very nature of love requires you to be vulnerable and trusting. Love is simple yet complicated. Forgiveness is simple, but the changed behavior that supports the forgiveness takes a while. Patience is simple, but continuing to be patient when the same wrong is being done takes time. Love is a dynamic back and forth flow of commitment and emotion. A hardened heart will either break at such movement of love or simply leak distrust all over. If you want to love again, keep your heart soft. From general acquaintances to intimate love, a soft heart is needed.

More importantly, a hardened heart towards another person is the same heart towards God. Denying that your heart towards man is the same as towards God is to agree to be a hypocrite. Jesus said, "Whatever you have done to these you have done to me." You see, God expects us to love others when we say we love Him. It is anti-God to say you love God but not love His people. When Jesus taught His disciples to pray, He told them to pray: "Forgive our sins as we forgive those who trespass against us." That is to say, God should not forgive you if you do not forgive others. It is truly a fallacy to believe that we can love God and dislike people. Your daily time in the presence of God prepares your heart to love people the way God loves them.

My relationship with God is so important that I am willing to forgive others and keep a soft heart. The consequences of a hardened heart are too severe for me to trade the presence of God for. It is only fair that I say this. The heart that refuses to be hardened hurts a lot more and longer. The hardened heart shuts out all love and all pain, to the point it cannot be hurt again. It cannot feel again. Conversely, the soft heart allows all the love and feels all the pain. That is the point of your dilemma: Do I continue to feel this pain believing that God is working in my heart to make me whole and bring me to better place? Or do I stop the pain and harden my heart, even though I know that is not God's best for me?

It is very unwise to put your healing process in the 5-step, 10-step, and 12-step program. I refuse to prescribe any such routine because I am not in control of what happens in the presence of God. He will take you on a journey that is customized for you. There is no use comparing yourself with others based on the length of the process and how they felt. You are unique and so is your healing. A good place for all of us to start is to get in to the presence of God. While you are there, be mindful to acknowledge those who hurt you, and forgive them. Wish them well and speak well of them. Don't leave his presence until it's all resolved.

Your answer is in the presence of God. Your healing is in the presence of God. I know you want to shut out everybody that looks like your bad experience, but that does not include God. Soften your heart and let Him in. Be healed in Jesus name!

6

LOOKING BACK

For momentary, light affliction is producing for us an eternal weight of glory far beyond all comparison." 2 Corinthians 4:17

YOUR TIME IN the presence of God will bring some significant answers and healing to your heart that no conversation with another person can. It is also true that the residue of the hurt and pain will take time to fully heal. The presence of God cleans the wound and makes sure no foreign objects, thoughts, or emotions remain. When that is done, the true healing begins. It may swell or puff up, but again, it is cleaned in the presence of God. Though you are spending time with God, the spot becomes painfully sensitive. Anybody who attempts to address or touch that spot in your heart gets a cold reaction or a soapbox lecture. You are still healing. Imagine doing all this without the presence and Word of God. Impossible! Get in His presence.

After a wound heals, over time, months and years, you are still left with a scar to remind you what happened. You feel good and harbor less pain in your heart, but for the rest of your life, the pain and its healing becomes a part of your story. Yes, it is part of your story. The good thing is that you can now share it and tell others how you overcame. It is time to go back to the prisoner camp and get others out.

To assist you in the processing of some of the situations you went through and felt like were hell, let's take a trip down memory lane. If these stories apply to you, thank God. Write down your stories. The power of sharing your story gradually diminishes the burden of knowing and carrying the load all by yourself. These are simple stories of how I felt my situation was too painful to bear, but had no clue God was preparing me. Smile, laugh and cry at these stories. Whatever you do, keep moving forward toward healing.

COMPULSORY FASTING

I arrived in the United States on December 6, 1996. The weather was chilly, and for the first time, I saw my breath. When anyone asked me what I was doing, and I responded, "Just chilling," it was most often very literal. A few months later, I was enrolled in TC Williams High School. The experience was totally different. Students were raising their left hand in class, and it was normal. Do that in Ghana, and you will feel the apocalyptic wrath of your teacher. Kids wore their own style outfit to school and some left nothing to the imagination. That was different for me because my high school in Ghana, St. Thomas Aquinas, required uniforms.

I was enrolled in school under the care of a legal guardian. My sister, brother, and brother-in-law were still finding their feet in our new country. I was never enrolled in the free or reduced lunch program, and being new to the country, we had very little money. I did not get lunch money. I was forced to go without food during school until late in the evening. That includes skipping breakfast. Forgive me, I was not skipping breakfast because I wish I had the option presented to me. It is difficult sharing this because when I was in Ghana, I never starved. If I did not eat, it was a choice.

Finding myself in this predicament, I did the only thing I thought possible. No, I did not beg for money or food. I fasted. When my friends raced to the cafeteria, I opened the side door and went to the track field. Thinking about it now, I wonder why nobody ever stopped me all those 17 months. It must have been a God thing - ALL HALL MONITORS, back off! I would walk around the field, Bible in hand, tummy growling, and a heart yearning for God. I worshipped and prayed. I would occasionally sit on the bleachers to read the Bible if I was not read-walking. It was during this time that God birthed in me the passion for establishing a Bible Study Club in the school - Restoration Christian Fellowship. It was on the track that my spirit yearned to serve my generation with the gospel of Jesus. It was also on that track that God proved my dedication and sacrifice. From the outside, it looked like a foreign student lost in a new country and new school and totally lonely. Au contraire!

Looking back, I realized that I had traded food for the anointing. I traded building friendships with peers for a divine encounter with God. It was then that I understood that being alone was very different from being lonely. I found ways to be alone, if only to talk with the love of my life, Jesus, for just a few minutes. What some would describe as child abuse was my season of preparation. It was the presence of GOD that helped me adjust to this new country. I needed my faith and faithfulness straightened if I was going to build on what I learned from Ghana. It was the one constant before, during, and after my relocation to America - the presence of God. You too are, in many respects, in transition. With your spouse, church, friends, job, etc., the one thing you can do to bridge the gap is to press into the presence of God. Stop looking for other things to fill your heart and mind. Face those giants with prayer. Confront those emotions and thoughts with the Word of God. Fight for your victory in the presence of God.

Every country and kingdom hopes that there is a smooth transition when a new leader arises. Friend, it cannot get any smoother than when we do not change governments. The same government means continuity. Keep connected to the King of kings. During your transition, don't change your allegiance, passion and commitment to Jesus. It looks lonely, but God is proving you for a greater assignment!

College Reject

I applied to college. I received the acceptance letter. I was overjoyed and excited. I was going to college. I was going to the Ohio State University. Ah! I could not contain myself because this was part two of the mission I came to America to accomplish. High school was done. It was time to step it up to college. I was ready.

I did not go to Ohio State University. I could not afford it—no FAFSA, no grants, no scholarships, no college. It was a devastating blow, enough to cause a temporary pause and reflection on the future. Would I make it? I knew I would, but the process was just getting started.

I graduated high school, and having no college plans for the next year, I joined the workforce. I began as a cashier at a grocery store. Then I added a sales associate job at an office supply company. I quit the grocery store and worked for another small chain company as a pharmacy technician. The days were long for me. That was my first time working, and I was pulling 14-hour days.

The physical pressure on my body was great. Whenever I sat, I slept because I was always exhausted. The only days that I remembered were Sunday (I was in church) and pay day (I got a check). All the other days ran together. The most difficult part of this time of my life was not the work, because I embraced hard work; it was dealing with the fact that all my friends were away in college and I was left working double shifts. I could not help but conclude that if my father was here, this would never have happened. My friends told me about the exciting things in college while I went to bed with the code for banana (4011) stuck in my head and replaying in my dreams. For a 16-year-old doctor to be, having never missed a day of school, this was getting pretty discouraging.

I continued praying and abiding in the Word of God because there was no other choice but to lean in closer against my Daddy's chest. He knew what I didn't, and my safest bet was to trust Him. My favorite song during this season was a song by Andréa Crouch titled "He brought me this far." My God did not bring me all the way from Africa, over the Atlantic to put me to shame. He would fulfill His word concerning me. The words of this song are so powerful that they ring true in my heart. I feel the words of the song as if they were my own:

> *He brought me this far*
> *God brought me this far*
> *And he's going to take me all the way*
> *I believe he's going to take me all the way*

Looking back, I realized that God was giving me a crash course in cross-cultural education before I got to college. All the clients I had to deal with on my jobs taught me how to relate and understand people and the American culture. I learned to slow down when I speak, otherwise my co-workers would not understand what I was saying. I learned the discipline of commitment and integrity—working hard when no one was looking and taking care of what belonged to another person. I learned how to save money, write checks, give my tithe, contribute to the home, help others, and be generous. I learned from my boss, Russell, that I was "a special kind of guy" and from a customer that I was "a scholar and a gentleman." This may mean nothing to someone else, but for me coming to America and trying to establish myself, it gave me hope. I may not have been fully acclimated yet, but I was on the right track.

Eventually, I was able to attend Mary Washington College, and like one administrator put it, I was "like a duck in water." I enjoyed my time in college, in a good way of course. My God did not leave me alone. He brought me through to graduation. Faithful is He!

You may feel left behind and delayed because of what somebody did. Everybody around you seems to be moving forward with their lives except you. It was not your fault because you made the grades and did your part. You stayed home to take care of your mum or dad when they felt ill. You forsook your dreams and goals to serve another person. You would do it again if you had to, but it hurt. Friend, your time is not wasted and your vision is not lost. You will begin and finish well. Regardless of the cause of your delay, you serve a timeless God who knows the end before the beginning. In Him, you lose no time. Be encouraged!

LONE RANGER

College was a blast, but like everyone, I had my down moments. I am very outgoing and can basically strike up a conversation with anyone. That meant that I had many acquaintances. I call them acquaintances because they did not know the man behind the smile. When I was struggling emotionally, they did not know because they were not close enough. There were others that I was close to. These were my Christian brethren. We prayed together, worshipped together, and studied the Word of God together. It was good.

A friend of mine, Janaye, approached me about beginning a Christian Student club she had on her heart. With her friends and some other students, we began Ambassador for Christ. It was great with growing pains. Janaye was a senior then, so the following year, she graduated, and I became the President of the group. After spending all summer long planning the upcoming year, I was excited to put things in place when the fall semester began. I scheduled an interest meeting and committed one of the unpardonable sins of ministry leadership. I had a long table of appointed leaders and had less people in the audience—too many chiefs. The other unpardonable sin was to appoint the people before I knew their hearts. I was so eager and excited to see the group succeed that I made decisions based on who I thought they were.

The disappointment to follow was devastating. I had to cut back on the number of chiefs because frankly, the chiefs were not leading. My worst conversation was with this girl I'll call Yolanda. I broke the news of her demotion in our Chemistry class. I told her, after much praying and thinking, "I have to drop you from the leadership team." Her reaction was classic: "Drop me, drop me? Am I a hot potato?" And the falling out began. One by one, my entire leadership team left, including my closest friend. They left the leadership team and the organization. I agree that I had immature leadership skills then, but I felt they abandoned me.

The other reason they left was because I began dating a girl from Georgia. I was a dark gentleman from Africa dating a white lady from the South. The connection was that she loved God, and that was my basic requirement. I had people that I once laughed with walk past me on campus as if I was a stranger. The gossips and the lies were constant. I would hear them leak out often, but the reaction towards me was so clearly that of rejection.

The Bible Study dwindled to single digits, and so did my friends. Though I had trained myself to be able to walk alone (remember the high school track field), I could cut this abandonment with a knife. My heart was bleeding, and no one noticed or cared. I remained faithful even when I was the only one at the Bible Study. Every Tuesday and Thursday, I was present to pray and teach the Word to empty seats. Gradually, the group grew again, but it was very difficult for me, personally. My hopes for the group were completely not what I was seeing.

To make things worse, eight months later, my girlfriend broke up with me over email. She had another suitor who was more welcomed by her parents than I was. Come to find out, she had been in hot pursuit of him the last couple of months of our relationship. It seemed like the one person I thought had more reason not to leave decided to leave me too. Tonto, where art thou?

Looking back, I realize the mistakes I made as a leader. The position does not make a person, so it is crucial to know the heart of the people before appointing them to any office. I was forced to learn the art of communication. "Dropping" someone off a team may be acceptable language in my mind, but it should never have left my lips. I promise you I have learned how to communicate better.

God was also proving my heart during those lean years. The life of a leader is simply lonelier than others. You make decisions that others would not want to. The results will surely not be accepted by all, so you always have someone to explain to and something to resolve. I sincerely believe that my faithfulness in the absence of people proved to God that I would be faithful when people showed up. You cannot be controlled by others. You must hold on to your convictions and honor God through them even if everyone leaves you.

My girlfriend left me because she could not handle the racial tension and pressure that came with our relationship. The perspective of her parents was very important to her, and I will not fault her. The result was disappointing, but I learned some very important lessons. I'll classify them under the safe category of "cross-cultural interactions". It was a lesson in global missions.

I thank God that my friends left me. I learned to trust God and value His affirmation above others. I thank God the Bible study diminished because I learned that success does not come overnight, and in the Kingdom of God, hard work and dedication still apply. Good preaching does not build relationships. Investing into others and truly caring about and knowing them is what builds lasting relationships. I thank God that my first girlfriend left me because my second girlfriend became my wife. Yes! I thank God that what felt like a soap opera experience was a teaching arena used by God to prepare me for today. Our church is multicultural for a reason. I was seasoned in the battles of multicultural relationship when I did not know it. God knew and my friend, He knows where you are. He is right there with you!

HOUSE POOR

My wife and I bought a house right before the housing market crash in 2008. It was all based on my spectacular plan of refinancing my student loans with the equity gained over time on the house. The plan was perfect until boom, the market blew up, and I was left with a house valued at less than I paid for it. Mind blown, strategy blown, and budget blown!

Wait, did I say budget? I take that back, there was just a mental note of what was due, but a written budget, no. A budget is not effective until two things are in place: One, you write it down and review it often. Two, you stick to it. What is a budget for if you do not allow it to direct your finances? So, I had no budget, and that was the doom of our finances. We had also taken on more house that we could comfortably afford. I made too many mental adjustments without backing them up with actual numbers.

We lost the house through a short sale process. It was the starter home of our dreams. My wife loved it and took great care of it. Losing the house shook my wife's confidence in my ability to handle the finances. She did not feel safe because I was careless and not intentional about saying no and controlling our expenses. I have had to prove over the past years that I was capable, and I have earned her trust again. Losing her confidence hurt me more than losing my house. I worked diligently to make her feel safe because I was honest about our finances, good or bad, and gave her full access and permission to review the accounts and ask me questions. She does not check the accounts, but she sure asks me questions to keep me honest and accountable. I needed to be held accountable, and that has enriched our marriage.

We moved into a rental home and began our rebuilding process. I read Dave Ramsey's books and listened to his educational CDs. I developed a written budget and stuck to it. I paid off debts that we owed and began to live within our means. There are still a few bills yet to be paid off, but the good news is that they are in good standing. That is important for a good credit score and history.

While I was getting my financial act together, we had our first daughter, and four months later, I lost my job. The problem now was not the absence of a written budget. The problem was that there was no money to fund the budget. There were times where I would look at the budget and try to trim it down to the essentials only. Still, our income was not enough. We were forced to move again—this time to a bedroom in my sister's home. Humbling? Yes. Necessary? Yes. I depended on gifts that people gave to keep us going. I did not beg, and I would not ask. I had to trust God to meet our needs, and He did.

Two of the most important lessons I learned during this time are actions I still take today. First, I kept tithing. A tenth of every income that came in belonged to GOD. My dire situation did not just justify defaulting on my tithe. I would be a thief if I reasoned my way out of giving my tithe unto God. Secondly, I gave intentionally to others. I knew the way out of my situation was to sow my way out. Whenever I found a need, and as I was led by the Holy Spirit, I gave. He who waters shall himself be watered.

Looking back, I would not have lasted long financially if I did not learn how to budget and spend money wisely. Though it hurt, I thank God I lost my home. When I had to move with my sister, I thanked God that she was there. They had moved down from Northern Virginia only a year prior. Talk about being sent of the Lord. I thank God that I lost my job because I saw firsthand that I need Him more than money. I acknowledge that He can meet my needs without me.

I hope some of these stories, in part or in whole, helped you gain perspective on where you are and the things you've been through. They were difficult, but thank God for them anyway. I resolved in my heart to live on God's Word and fully trust Him.

I made the decision that I will never beg or borrow another day in my life. I make this declaration publicly because I am fully convinced that I shall lend and not borrow. The borrower is slave to the lender. I am too blessed and too royal to beg. If I must go without food, I'll fast. If I need to ride a bicycle because I have no car, I will. I will not borrow. The powerful thing about this stance is that it moves and excites God. It is a declaration of faith, and faith pleases

God. He will honor you if you trust Him alone. He will defend you for His name's sake. It was hard, but He brought you through. It may be hard for you right now, but I am a living witness God will bring you through!

7

SIMPLY NOT READY

"Blessed be the LORD, my rock, Who trains my hands for war, And my fingers for battle." Psalm 114:1

WE ARE ACCUSTOMED to people around us making us feel better than perhaps we actually are. Their intentions are good; keeping us from feeling defeat and passively encouraging us to do better. The unfortunate side effect of over praising and not correcting is that we have become bigger in our eyes than we actually are. We consider any non-flattering comment as criticism when it is the truth we need to hear.

Most of the people around you will not tell you the truth because it will hurt, and they do not want to be the cause of that. Some of these people may speak the painful truth when it gets dire, but there are some who would not. It is important, therefore, to surround yourself with friends who will be honest with you. The number in this group will be small, and could be just one person, but make sure you have that one in your corner. The epidemic of inflated egos and unproven heroes is destroying our family, church and societal structures.

When we behave and talk like someone we are not, dishonesty creeps in. No, it is not faith to assume what you are not, and consequently deceive people. Faith is backed up by action. Faith without works is dead. It is pretentious when we portray an image of who we are not. Some do it to deceive others, but most of us do it because we have inflated egos that blind us.

When we face adversity, we may believe that the other party is guilty for the part they played. However, the greater perspective is that we were not ready like we thought we were, or were made to believe. We were made to believe that we were the best preachers they've ever heard. They told us we were so anointed and powerful. People were impressed with you, either publicly or privately. Eventually, you became intoxicated with the praise; you believed the hype and became entitled. I do not mean to infer that you were disrespectful and went around strutting around in a prideful manner. I am talking about the quiet whispers to your heart. Maybe once you were nobody, but today you have arrived. That self-praising undertone is dangerous, and the devil uses that to set us up for failure.

By the grace of God, I have been a leader since I was a child. I found myself always leading or directing a group of people. Most times, the position and role found me when I was not looking for it. I embrace leadership and enjoy serving other people. I came to the US, established a Christian Club in High School, another in college, and by that time, helped plant a church, all in the span of 3 years. Did it get to my head? No, because, in the moment these things happened, I did not realize the magnitude of each endeavor. On the contrary, it was the praise and accolades of people that made me feel so confident that I believed I could do anything.

I can remember the humbling moments that slowed me down— when I thought I should be moving faster and I needed a pause button.

My friends in college abandoned me and left me at the high table. I was leading with no one following. John Maxwell calls that a walk. I understand now that God was working on me, but when I was going through that time, I felt rejected. How could they? Did they even know who they were leaving? It's me!

The first message I preached in church in America, my senior Pastor told me, "You have potential." What? Potential? How dare he call me a work in progress? I have arrived, and I am anointed. He must have missed what God was truly saying.

I waited for over a year after my ordination as Pastor to preach my first message. After I was done, people said it was good; that is expected. After many years of preaching, a lady told me in casual conversation that I was doing well with the preaching. Wait for it! My preaching was good as compared to the first time I preached. She said she could not understand most of the message and that I sounded nervous. What!!!? People told me then it was good. I felt I was amazing. The truth was that it was just okay.

Before I was married, I felt I was the most patient and loving and understanding and prayerful man ever created by God. Any lady who refused my invitation to be my girlfriend would be a fool to miss such an opportunity. That was until I got married. Then, my super awesome patience that could not be moved sank—like the Titanic. The unsinkable ship sank, and I realized I needed help being a husband. Five years before I was married, I thought I was ready, but I wasn't.

The truth I share with you today is that you might have felt ready for whatever was in front of you. And missing it or being hurt by it made you feel robbed and disrespected. I acknowledge your emotion, and the truth remains that you were simply not ready!

Let's discuss some areas where you may not have been ready and may still need to improve to fully benefit from your past painful experience and to also take constructive steps to move forward.

LEADERSHIP INTELLIGENCE

The art of leadership is so complex because it is vastly dependent on context, purpose, teams, and ever-changing personnel and personalities. A successful venture in one environment could be a disastrous flop if one or more of these ingredients is absent or deficient. The most important denominator in leadership is you, the leader. You, as the carrier of the vision, the glue, the conflict resolver, the encourager, the employer, as well as the terminator are very crucial for success. Your leadership ability and intelligence is very important.

It is true that the organization reflects the leadership and will go as far as the leader goes. What is your leadership intelligence? My ability to lead a group of 60 students of elementary and high school age every Saturday was amazing for a 13-year-old. However, it did not mean I was ready to lead a church of 50 adults with the adjoining ministries. Over the years of several leadership positions in church and school, I realized that I was a terrible event planner. Horrible! I learned that the hard way and through various opportunities and many failures. What do you know about yourself?

Before we delve further into leadership intelligence, you should answer that question: "What do you know about yourself?" Not knowing your strengths and weakness could be a devastating flaw. You may think you are ready to lead something only to realize that you are not. The rejection you faced was key in preventing you from undertaking a journey God had not cleared you to take. Are you disciplined with your time spent in prayer, worship, and Word study? Do you know clearly the voice of God, and can you distinguish it from others and your own, especially when it is chaotic and noisy? Are you prone to pride? Do you need the approval of people to be encouraged? Or are you so independent of people's help and encouragement that you feel you need no one?

When you do become a leader in a field, you must accept that fact that prior experience only helps in our confidence and could be irrelevant in the new arena. It is your responsibility to learn and study who and what you are about to lead. I will go further and say you must serve and prove yourself in that context before you seek or assume leadership. This principle applies to business, family, church, etc. You cannot lead where you have not sown, and you cannot know what you have not invested time and faithful study in.

Is it possible that our failure was due to the lack of preparation or simply mistimed action? No matter how I felt back in 2006, I was not ready to lead a church in any way. My Pastor rejecting the idea of planting a second branch was good for me. It prevented me from being baptized by fire and pressured into something I was not ready for. Fast forward 6 years, and my Pastor's rejection of me catapulted me into a vision greater than me and one that I was then ready to lead. I have learned to depend on God. Those six years taught me how to lead people older than me. They taught me how to stand my ground and lead without fear, even if the idea was not popular. It taught me not to bring church work home because it will affect my marriage and family life. I learned not to believe everything I read in a book by a Christian expert. I learned that programming was not the true medium of ministry, but relationship is. I learned how to serve those I led. I learned how to allow them to take initiative and fail, even if it cost me time and resources. I became a pastor of the people because I cared for them more than I did their approval of me.

Leadership intelligence is tied to time and experience. Do not allow your current trouble and heartache to force you into an endeavor you are not prepared for. Do not start a church because you did not like what your former pastor did. Do not begin your ministry because you feel "it's time" and that you are ready to be revealed to the world. Nothing can replace time and experience. Neither can be fast forwarded. Wait, you are not ready yet! Pain is good because it points to where the problem is and needs to be fixed. Before we fix pastors, churches, families, etc., let's take time to fix where you hurt, your heart.

EMOTIONAL INTELLIGENCE

Several books have been written about emotional intelligence, and I encourage you to pick up a few just to familiarize yourself with the topic. Emotional intelligence involves understanding your own emotions, the emotions of others, and how to effectively distinguish both and use them constructively to guide thinking and behavior. Basically, your emotions are pivotal to your life and leadership. Politicians hire experts to help them portray the right emotion in every situation to maximize their communication to their voting audience. The right emotion expressed at the right time counts for positive votes. Unfortunately, many politicians have lost entire election campaigns because of a moment of gusto, over-expression, or a lack of enthusiasm.

Your emotional stability, during and after your season of trouble, will determine how you connect with others and prove whether you are truly healed. The rush of emotion you are feeling could include anger, guilt, bitterness, inferiority, resentment, rejection, abandonment, and loneliness. These are not exclusive of each other. My hypothesis is that you had other emotional issues before this current situation you are going through. There may have been an experience just like this. If those issues were buried away and never healed, your current trouble stirred them up. This time we cannot hide them anymore.

Dealing honestly and truthfully with how you feel about that person or situation is foundational to your healing. How do you really feel? Why do you feel that way? How much of this is them and how much is you? Are you willing to forgive? Are you ready to forgive? These are important questions that many people gloss over hoping that right behavior will heal their emotion. You can only pretend and even deceive yourself for so long. Eventually, it will show.

Let's go a little further. Have you mastered your emotions? Let me explain. Do you know what triggers set you off the wrong way? What buttons do people and the devil push that has you acting out against your will and what you know is right? Do you know how to control your emotions and not spill them over on to others? Are you able to hear about a friend's divorce after you've been through one, without pouring venom and anger into them as if it was your own? Know your emotions and train yourself to avoid the dumps. Allow yourself to be so healed that you can tell when an emotional trap is being set. The emotionally mature are not exempt from this trap. The traps will present themselves, but the ability to avoid the trap and diffuse it determines your emotional intelligence.

You are going or have gone through an emotional roller coaster. As you read this book, it's time for you to take time to pull out each emotion, reflect on it and let it go. For your own sake, it is necessary that you grow up and out of the finger pointing and blaming stage. Blaming others only weakens you because it removes the power of change from you and gives the control to something or someone else. You are responsible for your emotional health. It is time to move forward. Until you do this and receive a clear emotional bill of health, you are simply not ready.

I must emphasize that emotional intelligence in fully dependent on your truthfulness. No one knows the root and motivation of your emotions but you. People only see the fruit, but the root is known by you only. You may choose to fake your healing and display the right emotions. Sadly, no one will ever know the real you. Even worse, you wouldn't know yourself. It is an option, but please do not choose it.

Take the more difficult road of unpacking your emotions and allowing the Holy Spirit to heal you from within your heart.

A few days ago, I had a cleansing experience in prayer. As I was praying, God exposed deep rooted emotions of rejection and unfair treatment I had packed away. I had learned to shut it down. The comforting words and presence of the Holy Spirit helped me to forgive. He reminded me of who I was now and how my refusal to deal with my pain was showing up in my secret anger, thoughts, and behavior. I cried my heart out, asked God to heal me, and intentionally forgave. I feel better because I am better. I am healed not in my emotions but in the root of my emotions.

We are discussing your emotions because they led you to believe one thing; you were disappointed, and your emotions became more negative. Maybe you were not emotionally ready for what you wanted. Maybe you have not dealt with the past and present emotional baggage you carry. Now is your opportunity to do it right. Your destiny depends on your emotional intelligence.

Cultural Intelligence

Four months after my 30th birthday, I had spent an equal number of years in two distinctly different cultures. Globalization has made the world a smaller place, but cultures have not become remotely similar. Certainly, there are crossovers and multiple points of intersection, but the cultural pillars are still intact and vastly different. This unique balance of the African and American culture is empowering and does give me an advantage in understanding both worldviews and relating to others.

I would be naive to assume that I am most prepared for a global ministry right now based on my history. The world is a much bigger place than Africa and America. More specifically, the world is a bigger place than Ghana and Virginia. Our experiences are valuable, but there is a lot more to learn about cultures and people because even in our respective countries, we really know a lot less of other regions and people.

Cultural intelligence begins with embracing one's own culture and valuing one's history. Your history is very important, and though it should not limit you, you should not be ignorant of it. Your history is your story. Increasingly, our societies are blending, and many are choosing this new identity, but at the demise of their own identity. It is important to know your history and who your parents, grandparents and great grandparents were because that is what you bring to diversity. Dismissing all of that as old history strips you of your contributing power to any diversity and multicultural conversation. What you bring is what makes the interaction more fruitful and enjoyable. Make it an intentional goal to know your history.

Another necessary part of cultural intelligence is admitting and correcting your prejudices. Based on false information or negative experiences, we all have cultural biases. Examine your jokes and whispers. They are laced with stereotypes. Cultural intelligence requires you to mature and relate to people for who they are. Do not punish them for the sins of their fathers. Imagine if you were judged before you opened your mouth. Imagine if your appearance and history were used to settle a matter before people knew what was really in you. It is stooping low when we interpret what people say based on our prejudice. It is not fair, and it is culturally immature.

Apart from our physical and genealogical history, we are part of a much greater country, the Kingdom of our Lord and Savior Jesus Christ. How well do you know about the Kingdom of God and how it operates? There is much to be learned about the Kingdom, and your cultural intelligence of your heavenly kingdom will enhance your success in this natural kingdom. I appreciate the work and teaching of Myles Munroe. During his lifetime he laid significant ground work in understanding the Kingdom of God. I recommend that you study his messages and lessons. Apply them to your life and understanding.

It is easy to notice those who are genuinely proud of their earthly nationality but have a greater allegiance to the Kingdom of God. When they are hurt, their identity is secure because they know who they are. I must caution balance because it is very tempting to be so heavenly minded you cannot connect to us earthlings. Or you may be so passionate about your ancestral roots that you embrace their anti-gospel and anti-biblical messages. Either of those stances will create confusion.

The Church on earth should be a representation of what will be when Christ returns for His Bride. Different races and cultures will embrace and applaud different forms of worship and church expression because we respect our cultural backgrounds as we look forward to our heavenly worship services. When you grow in your cultural intelligence, you can worship anywhere Jesus is being exalted. You will not dismiss as wrong or unbiblical anything that is uncomfortable or not to your liking. Learn to go to the nations, literally and figuratively, and enjoy the diversities of worship. When you become culturally intelligent, you will no longer compare preachers so far as they teach the unadulterated Word of God.

You must worship where you are spiritually at peace and relationally connected because that is where God has planted you to grow. Outside of that, culturally intelligent believers are eager to connect with others different from them to learn and grow.

Can you see how your cultural intelligence would affect how you share the gospel? When we realize that sharing the gospel goes beyond one moment and could eventually require consistent encounters of discipleship, our cultural intelligence is challenged. Where are you unwilling to go because of what you have heard or seen? Are you limiting the Holy Spirit in your life because your cultural intelligence causes you to fear and therefore disobey God?

We soon realize that prejudice and stereotypes are not internal and secret thoughts. They affect how we engage and treat people in life. It impacts our relationships in the Kingdom of Jesus Christ. It could potentially keep you from destiny because you are unwilling to go past your assumptions. Ask yourself, are you culturally mature?

PEOPLE INTELLIGENCE

Joseph, Moses, and Jesus spent a great percentage of their lives learning to serve people who were not like them. Before the full manifestation of their destinies, they invested years of study and understanding the people they were called to lead. You cannot lead people you have not served. It may work for a while, but it will eventually lose its fervor. It is true that people don't care what you know until they know that you care.

Joseph, a Hebrew, was sold into slavery to the Amalekites and traders, and later sold into slavery in Egypt. The cultures and languages were different. The food and mannerisms were different. Though his cultural intelligence expanded significantly, Joseph still had to learn about the people to effectively minister to them. It is important to notice that Joseph was a form of a leader even before he left his family. His father, Jacob, trusted him with the reports from his brothers and the state of the flock. I believe his authority in the family business made it easy for him to share his dream about the sheaves bowing to him. Joseph had authority and the dream only emphasized it.

The level of leadership God had for him in Egypt made Joseph's time in Canaan a mere introduction to the life of a leader. God was preparing him to be second in command of Egypt. The training began at home, but it was perfected when God introduced him to the people he was going to lead. His leadership began with slavery, serving then supervising. In that journey, Joseph gained intelligence about human behavior and how to lead people from different backgrounds. Your situation is an introduction to People Intelligence. Where you begin is not where you will end up. Learn the foundations of relating to people and do not fall in love with the position. The position remains where you left, but the skills and understanding of people is transferable everywhere you go.

Many years after Joseph, Moses was born in a time when the new Pharaoh knew not Joseph. Moses would have had a different lifestyle and training if he was born in the days of Joseph. The closest to such a lovely season to be born would have been for the new Pharaoh to acknowledge Joseph and thus favor Joseph's people but he did not.

This sets up the course of Moses' most dramatic encounters in his life: the burning bush, facing Pharaoh and getting the tablets of the 10 Commandments. He spent forty years in Egypt learning how to lead and make his case to authority. He learned the meaning of leadership and what was most important in defending the lives of those he led. Forty years in Midian humbled him as he led stubborn sheep through a parched wilderness with limited supply. That was something he would repeat as he led the children of Israel in the last forty years of his life. At the burning bush experience, Moses learned the power and voice of God. He learned that God would defend His people. Moses received the tablets from God on the mountain, but was unfortunately forbidden to enter the Promised Land because he forgot this lesson: When it comes to God's people, you must do everything God's way. The people are only in your care; God is still their Father. Have people intelligence, but know that God's instruction unequivocally trumps what you or the people want.

Jesus knew that, so He did only what He saw His Father do. With the chain of godly authority established, Jesus spent 30 years gathering people intelligence. He spent all these years talking with all kinds of people: the poor, prostitutes, the Pharisees, the Sadducees, farmers, and tax collectors. He knew people! It makes Jesus' sacrificial death on the cross more meaningful because he knew the hearts of men and died in our place anyway. Or maybe He knew the hearts of men and confirmed why He had to die us. Either way, Jesus was not ignorant when it came to people; you should not be either.

The way to know the people is to serve them in their environment. Go to them, be like them, and give of yourself to them. That is the heart of a true leader.

In this chapter, I have sought to emphasize one crucial ingredient of your healing process. My aim is to alleviate the heartache that comes from believing you were robbed of an experience or that something you felt ready for was stolen from you. I empathize with your feelings because I have been there.

The only way up and out of that pit is to be fully trusting of the plans and purposes of God in your life. Without that perspective, everything we go through will be dark and without shape or form. The absence of God through your situation makes it chaotic and uncontrollable. But if you put God first in your life, His agenda for your life will remain true. I believe the words that John the Baptist spoke in John 3:27, in his response to his disciple's fear that John was losing followers to Jesus inevitably important. He said, "A man cannot receive anything unless it is given to him from above." What is mine is mine, and no one can take it from me. What is yours is yours, and if anyone attempts to take it, they will fail. Should you lose it, God will give you better. I declare in the name of Jesus that better is coming your way!

With the premise, I encourage you to shout, clap and celebrate Jesus. No need to cry or weep because God has greater and better in store for you. Whatever you went through will all work for your good. Rejoice, for you are safe in the Master's hand!

A humble and grateful attitude towards your circumstances saves you from promotion without qualification. There are many who have built edifices for themselves and taken on positions that God did not ask them to fulfill or appoint them for. It is a dangerous thing to be outside the will of God because you could not wait. It is an equally dangerous proposition to take a position without being ready for it. Your life and that of those around you will be jeopardized if you chase or cry over something that you were not ready for. I know you were convinced that it was yours and it was time, but in the eyes of God, you were simply not ready.

By applying that mindset, I never put a limit on what God can do through me. My potential is endless because I am never fixated on a position or a person. My life is in His hands, and He is a big God! If what I think I am ready for is only elementary in the eyes of God, He must have something more awesome and amazing for me. I thank God for trouble which revealed that I was simply not ready. And I thank God for the grace He gave to prepare me for the greater thing that He had in store in His perfect timing.

8

DIVINE HELPERS

"Therefore, since we have so great a cloud of witnesses surrounding us, let us also lay aside every encumbrance and the sin which so easily entangles us, and let us run with endurance the race that is set before us, fixing our eyes on Jesus, the author and Perfecter of faith, who for the joy set before Him endured the cross, despising the shame, and has sat down at the right hand of the throne of God." Hebrews 12:1-2

YOU ARE NOT alone in this journey. God is with you. God has ordained for you to succeed and be fruitful in the endeavor He has been preparing you for. Throughout all the trouble and pain you have been crying and wading through, He is preparing you.

"You brought us into the net; You laid an oppressive burden upon our loins. You made men ride over our heads; We went through fire and through water, Yet You brought us out into a place of abundance." Psalm 66:11-12

God is faithful to see you through and bring you to an enlarged place. Your confidence must be in the finished work of God. You will make it through this season. It is not a matter of if, it is a matter of when. It is also a matter of *HOW* you come out. I am not talking about you manipulating the situation and people being on your side. It is not about how you prove a point so everyone believes your story. *HOW* means the shape and form you are in when all this is over. It will be over, guaranteed, but your state of mind, heart and spirit will determine whether you learned and grew, stayed the same, or regressed in the situation. I pray in Jesus' name that you go forward! Go forward, in Jesus' name!

God revealed to me something that really brought confidence and comfort to me. The Israelites were in the wilderness, having left Egypt. Pharaoh decided he had made a bad decision to let them go, so he sent his entire army to pursue them. At the point of pressure and overwhelming helpless, Israel found themselves pinned between the Red Sea and Egypt's fierce chariots and warriors. To turn back was bondage, and to go forward, certain death. Or so they thought. I declare that you go forward in Jesus' name!

Israel crossed over the Red Sea on dry ground, but the Pharaoh's army was drowned. At the Red Seas of your life, when you feel you have lost or are about to lose everything, look to Jesus for He is about to make a way where there is no way. This is the revelation: Though Egypt was pursuing Israel to capture them, it was not so in the mind of God. Israel was on their way to the Promised Land, and Egypt was on their way to the Red Sea. They just happened to be going in the same direction. For a moment, it feels like life is about to get worse, only for you to lift up your head and see the salvation of the Lord. That which oppressed you is being destroyed in Jesus' name!

I challenge you to declare boldly that no matter what the enemy brings against you, at the point of the Red Sea, you will cross over. You will cross over in Jesus' name!

WITNESSES GONE AHEAD

The writer of Hebrews, in Chapter 11, had outlined the Hall of Fame of Faith and their great commitment to walk through with God, even in the direst or impossible times. They walked by faith, trusting fully the everlasting plan and will of God. He did not fail them, and He will not fail you! The writer now continues to encourage us that seeing these men and women of faith who have preceded us, let us continue to press on and run the race with focus and tenacity. Don't give up, for many have gone ahead of you and have done well. You will do well in Jesus' name! You will finish well in Jesus' name!

The stories of Abraham, Isaac, Jacob, and others serve as our divine helpers because they assure us that we can make it. We acknowledge that these men had failures and setbacks, but they pressed on anyway because of their focus and commitment to God. We have failures and setbacks and have decided to press on anyway because of our focus and commitment to God. It is good to know that you are not alone and that you are in good company. Their defeats, victories and decisions provide us today a guideline of how to navigate through the wilderness of loneliness, fear, abandonment, rejection, and bitterness.

The greatest witness and example is our Lord Jesus Christ. The internal and external battles that Jesus fought were unfathomable. Even before the cross, He felt the weight of pain and pressure with no way out. He would be betrayed by one of His own leadership team and disowned by the Council of Priests. He had nowhere to turn. Yet, it was only the beginning of birth pains. Jesus' tears in the Garden of Gethsemane were like drops of blood, and that was only the beginning! Need I mention the carrying of the cross, the spitting, the disfiguring of His face and body, the nails heavily driven into his hands and feet, the sword thrust deep into His side? He literally tasted the bitterness of His soul when they gave Him vinegar.

Remember Him, remember His pain, and remember His agony. Remember also that Jesus ran for a bigger prize and knew of a greater conclusion to the story. By reading and learning from His life, you too will finish your race. Regardless of the frustrations of the enemy and the wickedness of men's hearts toward you, you will go forward.

Declare boldly: "I will go forward, and I will finish well."

OUR PRIMARY DIVINE HELPER

Friends are good to share and to process our thoughts with, but they cannot understand the infinite possibilities of all that God is doing in your life. Their personal experiences are shallow wells of wisdom for your situation because God is working something peculiar in you. Their presence and prayers are important, but let me introduce you to One greater than they: The Holy Spirit.

The Holy Spirit is the greatest Divine Helper, sent specifically to you for the difficult and challenging days and moments you are going through. He is your confidante, your wisdom, and your comfort. He is your God!

Without going through a doctrinal dissertation about the Holy Spirit, I want to encourage you to personally know and experience the Holy Spirit. He is your best and only source of divine inspiration and power to overcome the emotions and thoughts whirl winding through your body and mind right now. True and lasting freedom comes by the Holy Spirit. He is the Divine Helper that knows all and reveals all truth. He will reveal the intents of your heart and put you back together again. He cleans and purges and renews. The secret to healing and continuing your destiny journey is the Holy Spirit in you. Get to know Him, love Him, depend on Him, and make Him your first love and best friend.

The advantage you have with the Holy Spirit is that He will reveal things you thought you knew in a different light, one that makes you see the greater picture of what God is doing. He knows not only your heart, but the heart of the person that hurt you. A new way of seeing yourself and a Holy Spirit-revealed way of looking at those that hurt you, changes everything. You now begin to see and understand the root of your pain. The lies of the enemy begin to fall away, and suddenly you begin to see yourself through His eyes. You are no longer forgotten, used, and abandoned. You are not useless and left to rot. You are truly special in the eyes, heart, and mind of God. That revelation and advantage only comes with the Holy Spirit in you. Before you call anyone else today, get into your prayer space and begin to call on the Holy Spirit. He is on your side, and He is your only source of healing and deliverance. Your destiny depends on this Divine Helper. Do not ignore or take Him for granted.

SECONDARY DIVINE HELPERS
Though it may be difficult to read and acknowledge this part, I sincerely encourage you to press on through it. Your next level of divine helpers is the Body of Christ. Your personal pain may be from Christians, and the thought of them or church as a whole may make you angry. You become suspicious of everything and everyone and commit yourself to a perspective of utter distrust. If you continue in that, it will ruin you. You will know if you are receiving from our Primary Divine Helper, the Holy Spirit, when your attitude changes toward the church and other Christians.

God is not the author of confusion, nor is His Kingdom divided. Justified as you may feel, you are wrong in believing that you hear from the Holy Spirit and can be in opposition to the church. The Holy Spirit and His gifts are poured into the Body of Christ. It is in the Body of Christ, i.e. other believers and disciples of Jesus Christ, that the Holy Spirit is manifested.

> "...with all humility and gentleness, with patience, showing tolerance for one another in love, being diligent to preserve the unity of the Spirit in the bond of peace. There is one body and one Spirit, just as also you were called in one hope of your calling." Ephesians 4:2-4

The Church or a Christian may be the source of your trouble, and the church and Christians are also the source of your full restoration and healing. The Holy Spirit's intention is to heal you and restore you back to your place in the Body of Christ. You were wounded and unable to either give or receive love from the Body of Christ. The Holy Spirit heals you, makes you stronger and empowers you to receive and serve the Body of Christ stronger than you ever did before.

CHANGE YOUR FOCUS

It is not about you! It is about the Kingdom of God and the Lord bringing His children home. Yes, Christians can be annoying and mean, but every family has their battles. Some battles are worse and have greater consequence than others, but there is nothing the Holy Spirit cannot heal and make right, if we let Him.

The body is jointly fit together, with every part supplying a crucial ingredient. If you disconnect from the Body of Believers, who will play your role? Picture this: the arm decides it has the Holy Spirit but does not want to part of the Body. It becomes a dislocated arm. Part of the body, via the Holy Spirit, but not connected via church. The Holy Spirit and church go together.

Before you get defensive, I do understand that the way the church in done in many places is unbiblical and downright demonic sometimes. If that is the case, your Primary Divine Helper, the Holy Spirit will guide and lead you out of there. Unfortunately, it may have not been the Holy Spirit who led you out; it was the persecution, trouble, unfair attacks, abandonment, and betrayal. The way you were led or pushed out cannot be your focus. Our focus is to get healed, strong, and quickly take our place in the Kingdom of God.

I encourage you to pray, search, and find a Holy Spirit-led fellowship of believers, with healthy accountability and oversight. No church is perfect, but there are many churches planted and directed by God. Find one and plug in because God has not changed His mind about the church. It remains the principal arena where God initiates and advances His Kingdom.

"Iron sharpens iron, so one man sharpens another." Proverbs 27:17

The right group of believers will both love and challenge you through to your destiny. Like the word of God, the church is a double-edged sword. The same word of God that heals and comforts also shreds sin and confronts evil in or around us. As Christians, we are human, and we are a family. Offense will needlessly arise, but our response is not to disown the family. We pray, address it, and keep moving together. In the event that all your attempts at reconciliation are rejected, pray for your persecutor, and move on to another local body where you can be connected, encouraged, and accountable.

Your divine helpers are the Holy Spirit and the Church. Change your mind-set about them both, and you will experience a greater flow of life and power. The Church is the principal body in advancing the Kingdom of God. The Holy Spirit is the Governor of this advancement. They go together.

I recently reconnected with a friend I truly consider a brother. He was good to me when I first came to the shores of America. After high school, we went to different colleges. He was a year ahead of me because I had to take a year off. Our interactions became sparse, though I still considered him one of my close friends. Our lives went in totally different directions, and sadly, I cannot tell you all that has transpired in his life, except he has a good job, a beautiful wife, and three children. He serves faithfully in his church and is very well respected. Our conversations these days are mostly about catching up and sharing experiences we both missed out on.

My life, like everyone else's, has had its amazing highs and terrible lows. Marrying the love of my life tops it all. Losing my father who was my hero, counselor, and role model was downright brutal. In between these experiences, I was so committed to my pastoral job that I nearly lost myself when I lost my job. I would classify those pitfalls as circumstances beyond my control.

During my troubles, I saw the manifestation of God's goodness. I lost the home I purchased partly due to mismanagement of my resources. My understanding of money back then was horrible -- no budget, no savings, and no future planning. Thank God I am better now because life would have been messier if I still thought about money like I did back then. The exciting part about that season was that I really saw the hand of God move mightily. Divine provision was a reality, with God meeting our needs through people and resources we did not have. It was a beautiful thing to see God fulfill His word, the same which made King David declare:

"I was young and now I am old, yet I have never seen the righteous forsaken or their children begging bread." Psalm 37:25

The downward spiral continued when I moved in with my sister into a bedroom with my wife and two children. From being a proud home owner, I now lived in one bedroom, where I was unable to contribute to rent or food. It was humbling for me because I realized that confidence in man is fragile. My confidence was no longer in my education, wealth, or social standing. At that point in my life, none of those were either helpful or important.

You may find yourself in a difficult season of life, but I encourage you, it will change for the better. God will make you a sign and a wonder, and He will take you to greater heights than you have ever imagined. Trust in Jesus, lean on the Holy Spirit, and never doubt the promises of God.

The one thing that I erroneously thought I had no control over is what I want us to focus on and be mindful of. We all have practical problems in our lives caused by circumstances beyond our control. **However, there is one thing that we all have control over: OUR CONNECTION TO THOSE WE LOVE.** No matter how troubling and devastated my life was, I should never have lost connection with those who were important to me. Should any of you be reading this today, I am sorry for being out of touch. Let's reconnect soon. Reaching those we love is not a circumstance beyond our control, especially in this digital and mass communication age.

PEOPLE WHO CARE ABOUT YOU STILL CARE ABOUT YOU

It is mostly true that those who care about you still care about you, regardless of the state of your economy. They want to hear your voice. They want to know how you are doing. They care for your wellbeing. Even if they are unable to financially support you, they will be willing to pray. They love you because of you, not because of your house, car or money. It is you they love, so no matter how much life strips those things from you, do not forget that the people who care about you still care about you.

DO NOT SUFFER ALONE

Often in hard times, we think we are alone, but don't forget you have many more people who still love and think about you

The plan of the enemy is to divide and conquer. We call it privacy, but in the scheme of the enemy, it is a ploy to separate you from the connections that will hold you up. Imagine if the hand was bleeding but was disconnected from the heart -- it will die off, and that is exactly what the enemy wants. Best case scenario, though the hand is still physically connected, it is functionally worthless. How many of your relationships are in this category – physically present but spiritually or emotionally defunct? This is a result of isolation. Hence, the Bible encourages us: *"not forsaking our own assembling together, as is the habit of some, but encouraging one another; and all the more as you see the day drawing near."* Hebrews 10:25

Do not suffer alone. Choose to connect, especially in the season of pain and frustration, because it is opposite of what the devil wants you to do and exactly what God will want you to do.

THEY NEED YOUR LOVE TOO

The blind spot of suffering alone is the ignorance of the pain those who love us go through as well. They yearn for the connection with you because you are important to them. My friend, for example, had tried through several means and opportunities to connect with me, but I was so blinded in my situation I could not see him or anyone else. I was lost in my world as I fought to overcome rejection, frustration, and abandonment. I bet you he was feeling the same way too. I undoubtedly believe that simply connecting with him would have been beneficial for both of us. Loving others is not a circumstance beyond your control. They need and deserve it.

To my fellow ministers in the vineyard, this is an exceptionally important decision you have to make. By virtue of our roles and responsibilities, we already suffer in silence. Our circle of trusted friends and confidants are limited. It makes it more expedient that the limited few around you are not marginalized, no matter what you are going through. In addition to the reasons mentioned above, your marriage and ministry depend greatly on you overcoming any attack of the enemy or life's burdens. You can therefore not do this alone.

> *"Two are better than one because they have a good return for their labor. For if either of them falls, the one will lift up his companion. But woe to the one who falls when there is not another to lift him up."* Ecclesiastes 4:9-10

I regret not knowing or thinking about it this way when I went through my seasons of adversity. Better late than never because I have purposed in my heart to reconnect and stay connected. I don't know about you, but I realize how many important relationships I have disconnected from using the excuse "life happens" or "circumstances are beyond my control." Life is not easy, but that is all the more reason why we must stay connected with those who mean a lot to us and who also are committed to doing life with us.

Simple Action Steps

STEP 1: Make a list of the 10 most influential people in your life

STEP 2: Honestly answer the question: "When was the last time you called them?"

STEP 3: Call or connect with them TODAY

STEP 4: Begin the process again with the next 10 most influential people in your life

> *"Like cold water to a weary soul is good news from a distant land."* Proverbs 25:25

You will be amazed at how a simple phone call or text will bring so much joy and love into your heart. Alright, go on now and reconnect with destiny! That is definitely under your control.

May you be healed by the Holy Spirit, for the Body of Christ, in Jesus' name!

9

GOD-DIRECTED RELATIONSHIPS

"A man of too many friends comes to ruin, but there is a friend who sticks closer than a brother." Proverbs 18:24

OVER THE YEARS, I have discovered and thus placed a greater significance on my relationships. Not everyone is meant to be major in your life, but that does not diminish their significance. There are some relationships in our lives that are toxic and anti-destiny. It is therefore paramount that our relationships are God-driven and not self-initiated.

The quality of the relationship is not how often you communicate with the person, but the degree of sacrifice shared between both persons. How far are you willing to go, and what are you willing to sacrifice to invest, grow, and keep this relationship? There are several key relationships in my life that do not require a daily, or even weekly phone call. However, in the most important moments in my life, I can count on them to be present, and I will do the same for them. The product of trouble is that it redefines our relationships and forces us to reevaluate which ones are worth keeping and which ones will not stand the test of time. An easy way to identity which one to keep is to answer these questions: In my moment of struggle, pain, and confusion, who is with me? Who is willing to be inconvenienced for my sake? Who is willing to sacrifice their time?

There are many God-directed relationships that are lost. The devil and his cohort of demons are most certainly active to disrupt any good relationship because of the obvious unity and fruitfulness that comes from it. God-directed relationships are also lost because we listen to the wrong or false reports about the other person. I have personally experienced this. In the time when I needed to be there for my niece, I allowed wrong counsel and fear to keep me from being the uncle she needed and expected me to be. It's been almost 10 years, and I am still rebuilding trust to hopefully reclaim what we once had. Then there are the relationships that are lost even though you did nothing wrong. You were misrepresented or misunderstood and a relationship you had poured your heart into suddenly dissolves into nothing. That is painful.

God intends for the relationships He brings into our lives to last. Again, remember that the value on the relationship is not in how often you call or text someone. It is that deep rooted place in your heart where you are willing to give it all to see the other person prosper and do better. For that sake, relationships should last and stand the test of time. The idealistic situation would be for our children to continue the God-directed relationships that He initiates in our lives.

THE POWER OF RELATIONSHIP

We are created and wired to be in relationship. Without relationships, we have no value because relationships provide the atmosphere to express our humanity. A transformer, no matter how great it might be, is useless if it does not transport electricity. It is in communication and relationship with electricity that the transformer finds its purpose. Your purpose is revealed, amplified and encouraged in your God-directed relationships. It is in our relationships that God prepares us for our destiny. It is humorous yet true that when you pray for patience, God sends you people. People become the atmosphere in which to develop and express patience. Relationships connect us in a way that reveals who we are and gives meaning to what we do. Every interaction, communication, and connection to such relationships simply brings down our value. I encourage you to see beyond the surface and reach deeper into the power of meaning that drives relationships. For example, making lots of money from a business deal that lacks character and integrity diminishes your value, no matter the wealth. A husband showering his wife with gifts and showing all signs of a family man diminishes his value when he watches pornography. Any relationship that does not glorify God and is not God-directed will eventually take away from you. The enemy is good at distracting us with ungodly partnerships that look good and reasonable in the moment but are completely void of the finger of God.

GENUINE RELATIONSHIPS

True friendships endure conflict and come out stronger that before. The idea of conflict is so terrifying to many that they try to avoid it. It is presumed that a conflict-free relationship is a peaceful relationship. That is false. Conflicts are truly moments of opportunity for growth. Conflicts reveal a few things:

1. CONFLICTS ARE PROOF OF INTERACTION.

In as much as they are highly uncomfortable, conflicts expose the gem that two or more people are actually in communication. Without communication, there will be no conflict of emotions, ideas, directions, and vision. Relationships that try to avoid conflict are not genuine because wherever there is human interaction, there will be conflict. The surest way to avoid conflict is to delete interaction. The surest way to a weak and non-existent relationship is to avoid interaction.

2. CONFLICTS REVEAL OUR INDEPENDENCE AND IDENTITY
Where there is conflict, we agree that two parties are expressing opinions that differ from each other. No two people are alike, and consequentially, we all see the world and problems differently. Herein lies the problem when there is no conflict: One party has acquiesced and submitted their uniqueness to the other. If agreement means unity, people agree with each by suppressing their identity. Genuine relationships do not hide individual personalities and opinions. The delivery can be taught and guided to be healthy and proper, but the content of an individual's thought must not be diluted or censored. When we lose our power of choice, we lose our humanity.

3. CONFLICTS SHOW THAT WE CARE
There are multiple situations we face daily that we willingly ignore because we honestly do not care. There is the expectation, though, that when you care, you must do something about it, and in our bid not to be bothered by solutions to a problem, we choose to avoid them. A co-worker's cluttered desk may be discomforting to our eyes, but almost all of us ignore it. We do not want the responsibility of cleaning it, checking back on it, or the merely weird conversation that will be seem like a parent talking to their child. You ignore it because you do not care at all or care enough. When we care, we do or say something. We are willing to have a disagreement because we care and are personally invested. Truthfully, the day you stop caring is the

day you start avoiding conflict. So, if you are in a conflict right now, it is an indication that you care about the person, or at least about the results of the situation.

Genuine relationships have the battle scars of conflict—encounters, that have increased the value and the bond of the relationship. All my priceless relationships have survived moments or seasons of conflict. A genuine relationship must be and will be pushed. It will be pressured by life situations to see who will come and defend it. If it is not defended, if it is left out in the cold, if we walk away from it, we send the clear message: WE DO NOT CARE IF IT DIES. Every relationship that has died in your life is so because you or the other party consciously or unconsciously stopped feeding it. You may have cared, but you did not care enough to sacrifice your resources (time, money, love) to keep it alive.

My sister and I have a great relationship. We have been through a lot together, especially in America. Most of the time it was me depending on her. Now, it's more of a symbiotic relationship. We encourage each other, challenge each other, and laugh a lot. The value we both place on the relationship brought us to that place of conflict. We questioned each other, "What do you think of me, or how much do you expect me to contribute to this relationship?" Without going into all the details, we expressed our concerns and frustrations. We did not leave anything in the bag as later ammunition or as fodder for personal lamentations. We aired it out. It got heated at times, but it felt good to be honest. It felt good not to walk on egg shells. It felt good to laugh because something was funny and not because it was the polite thing to do.

My best friend became my brother because in the moment of conflict, we cared enough about each other to keep investing. We dealt with the awkwardness and the pretense. We came out firing then we retreated in anger or into the "whatever" stance. We talked again, we sacrificed, and we did things that proved that we cared more about each other than about being right or winning the argument. Genuine relationships are a result of pressing through and overcoming conflict.

Some relationships can be good even when not experienced conflict. Upon a closer examination, however, you will realize that the connection has been outside of personal space. Also, there has not been enough interaction to bring you to that place of conflict. You are at a vantage point right now because you are prepared for it. Don't go looking for conflict, but in your understanding, be prepared to deal with it when it arises.

10

THE GOOD, THE BAD, THE VOICES

"Even in laughter the heart may be in pain, and the end of joy may be grief. Proverbs 14:13

THE DIFFICULTY WHEN going through a difficult divorce in life or ministry is the reality of denial. It is as if we wish it never happened, and we try to make light of it in order to cope with it. Deep inside, we know it is real, the pain and rejection are real, and the feelings of being alone and now "damaged goods" are real.

I tried to spiritualize it and take the Christian high road while I was hurting and broken inside. Leading up to my surprise layoff, I would have bet my last earned dollar that it would never have happened. I thought to myself that my Pastor and I shared a bond and stories too intertwined and strong for it to fall away. I was convinced we could weather any storm. So when those close to me asked me to prepare, I ignored it in order not to feed its manifestation. And then it happened. Spiritualizing does not make the pain go away. You must deal with the truth of disappointment. What was once appointed, no longer is. Healing comes faster when you allow the healing balm of the Holy Spirit to flow into your real emotions and pain so you can truly be healed.

Time does not heal all wounds. It buries it deeper; that's all. Forgiveness and choosing to live life and fulfill destiny is what heals wounds. Forgiveness cleanses it, and the new-found joy in fulfilling what God has planned for you, sews you back together.

The healing power of the Holy Spirit is real. Allow Him to love you through it all. You must admit your pain, though. You must acknowledge your frustrations and feelings of betrayal. You must see in the moment that your actions and decisions are not as innocent as they were before. It will be restored, but now you need to heal.

My experience was like nothing I had ever been through. My first girlfriend broke up with me over email, but that was not painful. Stop. That is not true. It hurt like crazy. I was so disillusioned that I had to shut down my work in the chemistry lab midday. I didn't want to blow anything up, you know. The truth is that when anything or anyone you care about deeply walks out of your life without your input or choice in the decision, it hurts. You feel like everything you had invested in the relationship went down the drain. You feel used and rejected. It takes time to find your real self again.

To be healed of this break up I had to admit that it was over. No matter how I much I *faith-ed* it, it was over. My good friend Micky was there. He took me out to play basketball to help clear my mind. Then I had to choose to forgive.

I went to church a couple of weeks later to ask God to heal my heart before I gave it to the next person I loved. This was a good prayer because she happens to be my wife today.

Accepting reality and the power of the Holy Spirit is what brings about transformation.

So, as I was saying, the pain is real, and when I was separated from my former church, my heart was gutted out. I tried to act all cool about it, but truthfully, albeit temporary, I felt without purpose. On Sunday morning I found myself at home. What was I to do on Sunday morning at home? I have never just taken a Sunday off from church. You can imagine the disorder within my soul. I was trying to make sense of everything. It was tough.

The side effect of my awful experience was that I made an unconscious decision to do everything opposite of what my former pastor had done. It was painful to see anything that looked or sounded like him. I would run the other way with my fingers in my ears. Of course, I did not notice this while I was doing it. It only came to me later, just like for you.

First, I was very convinced about the church being a center where everything originates and comes together; a place where lives are equipped and transformed to be sent out to expand the kingdom of God; a center that does not allow for compromise because it is focused on building and pushing believers to reach higher for God and in life. I bought into the vision so much, I believed in the name of Destiny Christian Center. That was the name I truly wanted, but my pain blocked me from doing what I wanted because it sounded like my former Church. I wanted no connection or memory of it. Thank God, our name Living Destiny Church is powerful and packs more vision than I had for the other name. It is, however, worth mentioning that my decisions and choices were greatly influenced by my pain.

Another thing I did differently was to select the color of our chairs for the church. I chose a set of three and submitted it to my team for their input. The color set did not have blue in there because it was the color of the chairs at my former Church. This may have seemed childish too, until I took time to reflect. My reflection revealed that the pain was so deep that things that should not be affected were.

Don't take for granted this part of your healing process. Look at your choices and decisions after your painful event and you will notice how far you run from anything that looked like the pain. Yes, I chose maroon over blue (which is my favorite color) because the pain was real. I had to admit that as part of my recovery. The Information Cards were "Connection Cards". Ours are horizontal because the other church had it vertical. Ours is printed on white cardstock paper because the other was on yellow paper. "Silly," you say, but these were clues to me finding myself again.

You must admit that you have done things not out of choice but out of need to be away from pain. When you allow yourself to see those things, your soul settles, and you begin to see how much you are sacrificing and losing for something or someone who walked away. You have suffered enough. You have lost yourself enough. It's time to find yourself again: Time to be healthy again; time to do things because you feel led by God to do them. Be healed in Jesus' name.

THE VOICES

The last few words my former pastor spoke to me in-person were that I was a good preacher, but I was unable to plant and lead a church. According to him, it just wasn't in me.

The one thing God removed from me quickly was the pressure or need to prove the above statement false. My intention would have been to please man and not God. Be careful trying to prove a point. If you give into this temptation you will miss God because He is not about sharing His glory, His people, and His vision with anyone. I have seen people play the churches and begin ministries out of the need to feel important or validated. God only supports visions and works that He has mandated. If it is not Him, you are on your own, my friend. That's dangerous because you will lose yourself even more, trying to do something not for God, but against another man. Not worth it. Don't do it.

Those parting words from him were only part of the plethora of statements he made that kept ringing in my head. The devil was more than happy to remind me of them when Church attendance was not exciting. When Church attendance was 13 and half of those were my family, believe me, those thoughts got louder.

It took about a year to fully clear my mind of those discouraging words. I had to ask myself why I just couldn't shake it off. It was because I respected the one who said it. I submitted myself to his leadership. I saw him as a father. He was my boss. He took me into his house when my home was not ready. He was generous to me. I had served him longer than any other pastor. He gave me opportunity. He believed in me (at least for 7 years). He taught me leadership.

The ending was horrific. It was a bad ending. But the journey was not all bad. Truthfully, the journey was a blast until 9 months before my departure.

Give honor where honor is due. Do not throw the baby out with the bath water. Your healing is genuine when you acknowledge the good in the person without feeling like you had to. When you can praise their good qualities without feeling like you betrayed yourself, then you are healing well.

I did not flow in the prophetic until I met him. Nobody really gave me the opportunity and upward mobility that he did. No one taught me the ins and outs of ministry like he did. Like my brother-in-law, Michael, said, "Seems like you learned what to do and what not to do." So, I thank God for trouble. Through it all, I learned a lot.

Your greatest challenge will be learning to hear the voice of God again without interruption from past or present influences in your life. Your trust-o-meter is unstable right now, and it's difficult to fully believe what you hear. You constantly question what is being said for fear of being lied to again or being deceived again.

People have ideas and are more than willing to share them. Not everyone who says "God said" is really hearing from Him. However, be alert and prayerful so you do not miss out on what God is really saying.

There are the good memories, and the bad endings, and the unlimited supply of people's opinions. Acknowledge them all, appreciate them all and let God lead you to His plan. It will take time.

"But He knows the way I take; When He has tried me, I shall come forth as gold." Job 23:10

May you come forth as gold!

11

ATTEMPT GREAT THINGS FOR GOD

"Truly, truly, I tell you, whoever believes in Me will also do the works that I am doing. He will do even greater things than these, because I am going to the Father." John 14:12

RELATIONSHIPS BUILT OVER years carry great value because of the experiences and stories they bear. The times we laughed and the times we cried is the glue that bonds our hearts together. I observed an interesting phenomenon in the first few years in America. In high school and college I observed the power of a cast placed on a hand or foot. It is obvious that an injury occurred, which naturally carries pain however, that cast become the center of love and support in a way I could never have imagined. Permanent markers of different colors express the affection of people in good wishes, happy faces, and cheerful art. If casts could talk, the stories from around the world would be fascinating – pain, support, laughter, encouragement, sleepless nights, inside jokes, limited movement, terrible drawings, and safety all wrapped in one place. Various experiences, extreme highs and lows in one moment of time, these are what enrich our human connectivity. It is true that the lower the valley, the higher the mountain. The disappointing moments in our lives make us appreciate and enjoy the exciting moments even more.

Based on this human inter-dependency, other people's actions directly or indirectly affect us. As humans, we need and thrive in community and relationships. By our interaction with other people, we become participants, victims, or partners in their activities. The truth remains that people (familiar or unfamiliar) and their decisions (favorable or unfavorable) do affect us. The effects may be minor and ignorable, or they could be substantially significant, enough to change our lives forever. That is the nature of life and the complexity of human interaction and communication.

Our close relationships leave the most impact on our lives. I will never forget my father's funeral celebration. It was a strange combination of the emotions I felt personally, and with my family. His death was not sudden, so we had a few years to prepare ourselves for it. It did not make it less painful, but at least it was not unexpected. Personally, I was saddened that my beloved father was no more, but at the same time I felt a mantle of destiny and responsibility descended on me to carry on his legacy. I was both weakened and strengthened. My family likewise experienced this dichotomy. Our father was no more, but in his death, we came together and united as a family. All the siblings were together in one place for the first time in 15 years. The combination of the joy of seeing each other combined with the reason we came was poignant. We can find both sadness and joy in the same situation, and neither takes away from the purpose of the other.

Amid my pain and feelings of rejection, my destiny was renewed and empowered. If I was never laid off, I would have never had the opportunity and nerve to begin something new for God. Good came out of the evil.

"And we know that God causes all things to work together for good to those who love God, to those who are called according to His purpose." Romans 8:28

As I mentioned in the previous chapter, when I thought I was fully recovered, I noticed certain reactions and reminders that confirmed that I am still a work in progress. The destructive actions of one man affected others and me severely. It is my encouragement to them and to you that we acknowledge the pain and disappointment, but recognizes that our destinies are still intact God still expects fruitfulness from us. Both the Apostle Paul and the Psalmist point out that even the most broken of us have our hope in the Lord and The Prophet Micah articulates the declaration that we ought to join in:

"But as for me, I will watch expectantly for the LORD; I will wait for the God of my salvation. My God will hear me. Do not rejoice over me, O my enemy. Though I fall I will rise; Though I dwell in darkness, the LORD is a light for me." Micah 7:7-8

The increased connectivity between people and cultures around the world magnifies both the positive and negative impact from other people's actions. A great speaker from across the oceans can reach families in rural towns of another continent. In the same way, an indiscretion by the same man reaches those same families just as fast, though it bears unfavorable news. The technology of the internet, social media, and television has shortened the distance between any two points in the world. We are much closer to each other, for the better and the worse.

Now is a strategic time to attempt great things for God. The distance between two nations, two cities, or two people has not been any shorter in history than it is today. Take advantage of this connectivity and attempt remarkable things for God. Arrange your life in such a manner that you are passionately pursuing God and daily attempting to represent His kingdom.

We have the terrific opportunity to introduce Jesus Christ to more people at one time than ever before. Technology makes up for years of language and cultural barriers. Technology makes up for some of the financial limitations that keep you from being a global trendsetter. There is no excuse not to surrender your life to the great adventure of glorifying the name of Jesus to all in the world through your gifts, talents, and calling.

"For the anxious longing of the creation waits eagerly for the revealing of the sons of God." Romans 8:19

Your pain, suffering, and struggle have all prepared and brought you to this place of decision making. Will you serve God and continue to attempt great things for Him, or will you shrink back and point fingers at your abusers? You are called for such a time as this. Make your mark on the generations of this earth. Your past is your history, but it is not your identity. Your past story serves as the fodder to light up your destiny. Your failures and disappointments are important ingredients to your greatness. Do not allow any of it to hold you back.

There is so much work to do that you cannot afford to hold back. Get up and let's go! Let's remember all that we've been through and make the devil pay for it. Your choice to move forward and attempt wonderful things for God is an indictment on the enemy. It is a clear signal that whatever he intended to steal, kill, and destroy your life has failed. Punish the enemy by obeying and attempting great things for God. You refuse to give up, cave in, and quit. You will recover all and more.

In 1 Samuel 30, David was not yet king when he was faced with the devastating loss of his family and the family of the men with him. Everything they had at Ziklag was looted and the rest set on fire by the Amalekites. From a distance, they saw what would be the last thing anyone wants to see when returning from a journey: bellows of smoke from the direction and location that they called home. David's journey and his new reality was not independent. His men had sacrificed everything to be with him as he ran from King Saul to preserve his life. David's loss was also their loss. They too lost everything in the fire.

Their loss was so great that they wept until there were no more tears or strength left in them. The situation turned dire when they realized the cost of their commitment to David meant his loss was their loss and they had lost everything. They wanted to kill him. The desperation was real. David, as the leader, had to carry his grief and that of his soldiers. Such a task is overwhelming and could crash any leader, except with God help -- and He did when David encouraged himself in God.

The scripture is not clear how David encouraged himself but I conclude that encouragement came from seeing, hearing, or knowing something favorable. I propose to you that David considered his past and remembered the moments he faced the bear and lion, the spear of King Saul, and the giant Goliath. David noticed that in moments when he had lost everything, or seemed to have lost everything, God delivered him. There was nothing David had faced that God had not protected him from or provided for him overcome. Even in the land of the Philistines, where David sought asylum, God kept him.

I pictured David repeating and applying the same truth and principles he used when he encountered Goliath. Goliath came with muscles, height, strength, swords, shields, and a raucous Philistine army. The army of Israel was terrified every time the nine feet tall Philistine giant came bellowing challenges at them and the God of Israel. David showed up on the scene with an audacity of faith that defied his lack of military experience and insight. This is an excerpt of the Bible account:

> David: "Let no man's heart fail on account of him; your servant will go and fight with this Philistine."
> Saul: "You are not able to go against this Philistine to fight with him; for you are but a youth while he has been a warrior from his youth."
> David: "Your servant was tending his father's sheep. When a lion or a bear came and took a lamb from the flock, I went out after him and attacked him, and rescued it from his mouth; and when he rose up against me, I seized him by his beard and struck him and killed him. "Your servant has killed both the lion and the bear; and this uncircumcised Philistine will be like one of them, since he has taunted the armies of the living God."

When faced with a devastating situation in his life, David recalled his battle with the lions and bears, and the victorious confrontation with Goliath. The memory of these events remind David that God is with him and that he is assured of another triumphant ending. He felt encouraged! After enquiring of the Lord, David pursues, overtakes the Amalekites and recovers all. You will recover it all, in Jesus name!

This may be a time to cry and mourn. Take time to do that and while you are in that place remember the goodness of the Lord, and the victories He gave you, and encourage yourself in these things. The Kingdom of God needs you to pursue, overtake, and recover.

The gifts and callings of God in you are needed in the Kingdom. The wisdom from your painful experience is desired. Your presence is demanded. After the sadness and reflection, arise and attempt great things for God. No bear, lion, giant, Amalekite, loss of family and resources, or threat from friends who want to stone you will keep you down. Rejoice and encourage yourself because greater things await you.

12

THANK GOD FOR GOLIATH

"Give thanks in every circumstance, for this is God's will for you in Christ Jesus." 1 Thessalonians 5:18

A DRAMATIC ENTRY TO the main stage worth reviewing is that of David. He was a ruddy shepherd boy who simply loved God. In obedience to his father, Jesse, David lovingly provided for and protected the sheep. He killed bears and lions and did the dirty work in the family that no one wanted to do. I believe David did not mind because he got time away from his brother's weight lifting sessions, and it allowed him time to play the harp and sing songs to Yahweh.

While he was away, he was almost forgotten. One day, without notice, the prophet Samuel came to anoint the next king of Israel in Jesse's home. Jesse had to be asked if he had another son before he remembered David. His appearance and mannerism did not qualify him to be invited to the interview, so his father thought. God thought otherwise.

But the LORD said to Samuel, "Do not look at his appearance or at the height of his stature, because I have rejected him; for God sees not as man sees, for man looks at the outward appearance, but the LORD looks at the heart." 1 Samuel 16:7

The private anointing of David meant he was almost King of Israel. His new appointment did not have a start date. Imagine being hired for a job, but you have to keep the interview a secret, and you do not know when the job will start. Practically speaking, someone was already doing the job, and if they found out you were promised their job, they would kill you. That was the emotional turmoil this anointing caused for David. He went back to his shepherd duties as the next King of Israel, not knowing when, how, and why he would ascend the throne. What would have been a graduation for others was, to David a new beginning. It was the start of a journey he did not choose to embark upon. The calling found him. The assignment was placed on him. He now had a charge to keep.

During this waiting period, David was almost murdered. Not only was the mental torment of being the next king heavy on him, he had to play the harp for Saul, the current King of Israel. Saul was going crazy and needed someone to calm him down. This temporary relocation was going well, until David had to dodge a javelin from the king. Thank God Saul missed.

Israel was at war with the Philistines, and David was presented an opportunity to be a hero. I can only imagine the initial conversation between David and Saul when they met again after the javelin missed. David was, however, ready to lay down his life down to defend the name of His God. That was all he had ever known. Rather than go as his brother or Saul would, in armor and with sword, David went out to fight as himself. David understood that he and God were an army greater than any army on earth. On this day, every lesson from being a shepherd had come together, this time for a greater purpose: to protect Israel and defend the name of God.

> *"Your servant has killed both the lion and the bear; and this uncircumcised Philistine will be like one of them, since he has taunted the armies of the living God." And David said, "The LORD who delivered me from the paw of the lion and from the paw of the bear, He will deliver me from the hand of this Philistine." 1 Samuel 17:36-37*

GOLIATH'S DAVID

David did not ask for Goliath, but this giant came to him, and David was ready. The processing of God does not make sense, but obedience to God is still required. You do not know the future, but God does, so it is important to be obedient to Him, even when you do not understand. David was anointed King, but the next level was not the throne; it was to fight Goliath. We face tough situations daily, but one of them will be the culminating exam for the next level. Are you complaining about preparing for and taking the test? Are you frustrated because you think you are ready for the throne when God knows you are not? Are you angry at Samuel and calling him a false prophet because it's taking too long? Or are you still angry at your father and brothers for forgetting to invite you to the first meeting with Samuel?

Without Goliath, David is not known. Friend, Goliath was not an accident! David's encounter with him was not because he happened to deliver food to his brothers on the battlefield. God set up an appointment for David to meet Goliath. You have an appointment with Goliath. You can whine about it, cry about it, or step up to the opportunity. The very things you are railing against are the very things that set you up for greatness. It is undoubtedly painful, and it is time to turn that around for your good.

I needed to be booted out. I would have been comfortable taking care of sheep with the anointing of a king. However, there is a greater demand for my service. God said it was time to build, and whether I agreed or not was not important. I did not choose the sad and painful exit, but it happened. It had to happen.

Police officers have pepper spray in their eyes and their bodies shocked with a stun gun during their training so they understand the power of the force they bear. Similarly, how was I going to be a pastor of pastors and restore those who have been hurt and abandoned if I did not go through what I went through? I understand when someone says, "I was rejected." I don't sympathize, I empathize with the one who was unceremoniously cast aside. I have been there.

I thank God for my Goliath. You should do the same.

FAMOUS TO FUGITIVE

David dealt with Goliath swiftly, and as a result his reputation in Israel changed swiftly:

> *The women sang as they played, and said, "Saul has slain his thousands, And David his ten thousands." Then Saul became very angry, for this saying displeased him; and he said, "They have ascribed to David ten thousands, but to me they have ascribed thousands. Now what more can he have but the king-dom?"* 1 Samuel 18:7-8

The people loved David. David loved the people. David more importantly was beginning to see to the purpose of God coming together.

He is not king yet, but he feels like one. Everywhere he went, it was "David, David, David!"

No sooner had David began to enjoy his new place as hero, than Saul reminded him who was king. David was now a fugitive. He came so close to the throne and to the experience of feeling like a king. But he was not ready. God knows our hearts and is acutely aware of when we are about to settle and be comfortable. He moves us on quickly before we can put pictures up on the wall of our new palaces. He introduces a new challenge, an inconvenience, or trial we would say. That is God's way of protecting us from settling at any point that is not our destiny – or our destination.

'For My thoughts are not your thoughts, nor are your ways My ways,' declares the LORD. Isaiah 55:8

The thought of seeing His children resting in Lo-debar (no pasture) is so appalling to God that He'll use whatever and whomever to move you along the path of greatness He has planned for you:.

"For I know the plans that I have for you," declares the LORD, "plans for welfare and not for calamity to give you a future and a hope." Jeremiah 29:11

David was now a fugitive from the law. He was running from cave to cave, afraid for his life. Running through his mind were the same thoughts you may be having: "What did I do wrong? Where did I miss it? I only wanted to serve, is that wrong?"

In this part of his preparation to be king, David embraced the presence of God. It was in these lonely, dark nights that he wrote some of the most poignant psalms to God. These songs placed him right back into the moments he had with God when he was a shepherd:

"Even though I walk through the valley of the shadow of death, I fear no evil, for You are with me; Your rod and Your staff, they comfort me." Psalm 43:4

When he was tired and discouraged, he encouraged himself:

"Why are you in despair, O my soul? And why are you disturbed within me? Hope in God, for I shall again praise Him, The help of my countenance and my God." Psalm 43:5

When he struggled with the persecution he was going through, he confessed:

"It is good for me that I was afflicted, that I may learn Your statutes." Psalm 119:71

What you are going through may be difficult, but I encourage you to find yourself in the presence of God. Anger, bitterness, and revenge only make your heart harder and insensitive to God. Rest in the confidence that God loves you. May you see everything --the good and the bad-- through the lens of a loving father.

FROM THE CAVE TO THE CASTLE

Finally, more than 15 years, most of it spent running, hiding, and trying to stay alive, David was now king! Everything he learned from the tough times he applied as a ruler. David won great battles for Israel and brought peace to the land. He made mistakes when he forgot the presence of God and was distracted by the things around him. However, he was quick to return to his source of strength and identity God. The exciting testimony is that God called him a man after His own heart.

God never forgot the tender little shepherd boy who worshipped Him. David did everything because He loved God. Even in affliction, he still had a soft heart toward Yahweh. In his sin, David did not care if everything was taken. All he wanted was the presence of God.

"Do not cast me away from Your presence, and do not take Your Holy Spirit from me." Psalm 51:11

These scriptures truly summarize the life of David:

"He also chose David His servant And took him from the sheepfolds; From the care of the ewes with suckling lambs He brought him To shepherd Jacob His people, And Israel His inheritance. So he shepherded them according to the integrity of his heart, And guided them with his skillful hands." Psalm 78:70-72

Integrity means wholeness. Whatever happened to you was devastating, but you cannot sacrifice the wholeness of your heart. Keep your heart soft toward God.

Secondly, David learned to use the sling and stones, then the sword and spear, then wisdom and understanding. At every point of your journey, there is wisdom to be gathered, skills to be learned. Do not waste the season.

LEAVING A LEGACY

At the end of David's life, the most important thing to him was not his reputation. He was most interested in building a temple for God. It would have been his greatest honor and achievement. Though God would not allow him to fulfill this dream, David moved on quickly to empower and equip his son Solomon to build the temple.

He made him king and gave him all the resources needed to complete the work.

Your legacy will not be found in the vengeance you might take on those who hurt you. Your legacy will not be entirely based on what you built and did. In the eyes of God, your legacy is determined by what you pass on to your children. David told Solomon:

> *"As David's time to die drew near, he charged Solomon his son, saying, "I am going the way of all the earth. Be strong, therefore, and show yourself a man. "Keep the charge of the LORD your God, to walk in His ways, to keep His statutes, His commandments, His ordinances, and His testimonies, according to what is written in the Law of Moses, that you may succeed in all that you do and wherever you turn."* 1 Kings 2:1-3

> *"As David's time to die drew near, he charged Solomon his son, saying, "I am going the way of all the earth. Be strong, therefore, and show yourself a man. "Keep the charge of the LORD your God, to walk in His ways, to keep His statutes, His commandments, His ordinances, and His testimonies, according to what is written in the Law of Moses, that you may succeed in all that you do and wherever you turn."* 1 Chronicles 28:9-10

What heart would you pass on to children, a whole soft heart toward God or a hardened and bitter one? Their walk with God is riding on the condition of your heart. Your natural and spiritual children need you whole and healed. What say you?

I am excited about how far God has brought me, up from the pit of despair and hopelessness. It is my hope and prayer that you take this journey to healing with a heart set on knowing Jesus and abiding in His presence. You will see the hand of the Lord at work in every area of your life. I pray that you rejoice in your redemption story. Your history is your story, and the pain, struggles and disappointment make you who you are. No regrets, no shame and no fear!

I need you for the Kingdom of God. I leave you with two of my favorite verses in the Bible. No matter how you feel or where you find yourself, good or not so good, remember this:

"Though the fig tree should not blossom And there be no fruit on the vines, Though the yield of the olive should fail And the fields produce no food, Though the flock should be cut off from the fold And there be no cattle in the stalls, Yet I will exult in the LORD, I will rejoice in the God of my salvation. The Lord GOD is my strength, And He has made my feet like hinds' feet, And makes me walk on my high places." Habakkuk 3:17-19

Rejoice in the Lord always. I will say it again: Rejoice! Philippians 4:4

God guided you through difficult and devastating seasons of your life. The discomforts in those times were real, enough for you not to wish it on another. Nonetheless, we can and must thank God for the Goliaths we fought.

On the other side of conflict is a victory parade. A parade not only for you, but for all the souls you bring into and serve in the Kingdom of God. O, what a celebration that will be! Arise and overcome the dissatisfaction with man, and let's attempt great things for God. I will be waiting, my friend! I'll be expecting you!

THE AUTHOR

Rev. Moses S. Asamoah, Jr. is an Executive Coach, Organizational Consultant and Motivational Storyteller. He is the Founding and Senior Pastor of Living Destiny Church in Norfolk, VA. He is passionate about church planting, evangelism, proper spiritual order, the sound teaching the Word of God, and the empowering of all believers to discover, develop and fulfill their divine destinies. Rev. Asamoah served as Executive Pastor prior to planting Living Destiny Church. He has also served at various times as Youth, Associate, and Senior Associate Pastor.

Rev. Asamoah is the last of seven children, with two of his brothers serving as Senior Pastors in Ghana. Brought up in a Christian family, he devoted his life to Jesus at the age of 14. From that point on, God has systemically grown and developed him into His servant in the ministry. The greatest impact on his life was his father Moses Blackwell Asamoah. From his father, Moses has learned the true meaning of Fatherhood, and wants the true experience of knowing God as Father for everyone in the body of Christ.

He earned a Master of Divinity, and a Master of Arts in Organizational Leadership from Regent University, VA. Rev. Moses Asamoah, Jr. is the author of *Sweetly Broken: Understanding the Pathway to Your Divine Assignment.*

He lives in Virginia Beach, VA with his precious wife Delali and three beautiful daughters.